PORTRAIT OF
CARNEGIE HALL

PORTRAIT OF CARNEGIE HALL

*A NOSTALGIC PORTRAIT IN PICTURES
AND WORDS OF AMERICA'S GREATEST
STAGE AND THE ARTISTS WHO
PERFORMED THERE*

by THEODORE O. CRON
and BURT GOLDBLATT

THE MACMILLAN COMPANY · *NEW YORK*
COLLIER-MACMILLAN LTD. · *LONDON*

The Macmillan Company, New York

Collier-Macmillan Canada, Ltd., Toronto, Ontario

Library of Congress catalog card number: 63-14192

Printed in the United States of America

DEDICATED TO
ALL THE CHILDREN FOR WHOM
THE HALL STILL STANDS

Contents

Introduction

If CARNEGIE HALL has been an expression of our democracy for more than seven decades, it can be said that the eleventh-hour turmoil that saved the old place from demolition was itself an object-lesson in how our society conducts its business—and its art.

The furore over the razing of the Hall arose when Robert Simon, Jr., citing stockholder unrest in his real estate corporation, agreed to tear down the Hall, sell off the plot, and thus rid his company of an unprofitable burden. A variety of potential buyers turned up with plans for the site, ranging from a parking lot to a fire-engine-red skyscraper. But these plans never materialized, so Simon set a deadline for the disposition of the property: mid-1960. The year 1959, therefore, was spent largely in protestations against Simon by those to whom the Hall was dear—and in renewed protestations by Simon that he had no alternative.

A number of groups were formed to save the Hall; they came and went quickly, accomplishing little more than keeping alive the controversy in the press. In the Hall itself, a tenants' committee worked from within, while tenant Richard Schulze organized the Carnegie Hall Fund, Inc., to rustle up the several million dollars needed to buy the property. Another tenant group—the Telemann Society—turned out mimeographed broadsides and organized sidewalk demonstrations. Further drumfire was maintained by random individuals and groups parading on Fifty-seventh Street before and after performances in the Hall.

By the winter of 1959-60, hopes had dimmed; despair was setting in. One snowy evening, Jacob M. Kaplan, his wife, Alice, and concert violinist Isaac Stern discussed the situation in the Kaplan home. Stern was bitter about the imminent loss of a great auditorium and reviewed for his friends the many important reasons why this must not happen. Kaplan was moved by his friend; shortly thereafter he asked the executive of his J. M. Kaplan Fund, Raymond S. Rubinow, to look into the matter. Rubinow, a seasoned agent for public causes, set up a meeting with Jack deSimone (a friend and colleague who directs the philanthropic activity of financier Frederick W. Richmond), Mrs. Claire Feit (another friend whose life was an embodiment of the New York musical scene), and Stern himself. The January 10, 1960, meeting was informal, with neither agenda nor minutes; but it did produce a unanimity of opinion—Carnegie Hall *must* be saved and *should* be saved and this quartet would try to do so.

During the rest of the month, a plan of action was developed. Rubinow knew that time was too short to mount the kind of drive necessary to raise millions of dollars. He also knew that New York's leading individuals and foundations were deeply committed to supporting the Lincoln Center project, a complex of halls and theaters in the West Sixties which would replace a square mile of dank slums. He argued that a different approach was needed to save Carnegie Hall—a government-aid approach. Of course, federal aid was out of the question; about the only thing the federal government could do was to send up a photographer from the Department of the Interior to capture the place on film before it was torn down. The city of New York did not possess the legal power to seize the property—no matter how equitably it might compensate the owner—because no question of urban renewal or low-rent housing was involved. The state of New York, for political as well as legal reasons, could not step in as the savior of the Hall either. Yet, there was a loophole whereby Carnegie Hall might in fact find a lease on life.

The state of New York had already passed the so-called Bard Act, in which certain conditions were set forth for the saving of historical monuments from the Great American Bulldozer. If the Bard Act could be amended to allow the city of New York to condemn the Hall and purchase it for simple reasons of history and conscience, then it could be saved. This seemed to be the solution—except that it involved dealing simultaneously with a Republican state government and a Democratic city government in an election year. Rubinow, deSimone, Feit, and Stern saw that their tiny base would have to be broadened, that art and politics would have to be combined into one of those special American devices called "the balanced committee."

On February 7, 1960, in the home of Mr. and Mrs. Kaplan, a large yet select group of individuals gathered to become the Citizens Committee for Carnegie Hall. Labor, law, music, Democrats, banking, the press, youth, Republicans, racial and religious minorities, and sundry other segments of the body politic were represented. At this meeting a specific plan to save the Hall was unveiled and a few key people were added to the command staff: Vera Stern, the violinist's charming wife; Colonel Harold Riegelman, a lawyer well versed in city and state affairs; and deSimone's employer, Frederick Richmond. This was the "hard core" of the Citizens Committee and it deserves a second glance, for it is almost a case-study example of a community group formed to move the local "power structure" and, hence, organized to reflect that very structure.

In the lead—though often away on tour—was the energetic, impassioned genius of the violin

Isaac Stern, a Hurok artist who hasn't played to an empty seat in twenty years and whose personal knowledge of Israel and eastern Europe alone endeared him to half of all New Yorkers.

Close behind was Rubinow, the Committee's chairman, a respected reformer whose main concerns had been civic action and the community needs of Greenwich Village, where influential artists and writers still abound and where Tammany Hall, the hermeneutic center of New York's Democratic party is located. From this vital center, Rubinow had developed excellent rapport with the city powers—a rapport that had proved useful in the civic battles of Washington Square and Shakespeare in the Park.

Jack deSimone, Richmond's aide-de-camp and himself the possessor of a broad circle of well-placed friends, gave the Citizens Committee its necessary administrative stability and timetable responsibility—and its first-rate public relations program. As the administrator, also, of Young Audiences, a program which brings serious music into the schools, deSimone could draw upon the advice and support of friends in the fields of music and public education.

Jacob Kaplan not only gave the sympathetic hearing to Stern's cause that led him to launch the effort; he also provided for its initial financing.

Frederick Richmond not only brought financial help to the Committee, but, as a personal friend of Mayor Wagner and as chairman of the board of the Urban League (a national Negro service organization), Richmond fed additional strength and information into the day-to-day tactics of the Carnegie campaign.

The two women—Claire Feit and Vera Stern —did the tough paper and phone work and, —with customary intuition, corrected the errors in word or act committed by the hard-running, tie-flying men of the group.

Colonel Riegelman, who had been jurisconsult to Rubinow in the past on matters of the public good, took care of such necessary details as the incorporation of the Citizens Committee, advised it on the disposition of its funds, and drafted the bill which the state would have to pass if the city were to rescue the Hall.

(The colonel had once dutifully carried the Republican banner as candidate for Mayor of New York. He lost.)

Whether by accident or design, this committee—unlike the dozen or more other groups which came and went at this time in the cause of Carnegie Hall—had the special chemistry and diversity of talent that gets things done.

Three key actors were drawn into the picture in early spring: Democratic Mayor Robert F. Wagner, Republican State Senator MacNeil Mitchell (in whose district the Hall stands), and Republican Governor Nelson A. Rockefeller. These three had to do the final political-legislative work—and to encourage them, to build a climate in which they could accomplish this work, the Citizens Committee's little mimeograph machine spewed out a daily stream of press releases and manifestoes, quotes from leading artists and politicians, and a general quickening of a rhythm of success: "Never before in history has it been so important to remember that the Beethovens and Paderewskis of the future live among the struggling young men of today!" and so forth. Out-of-town friends lent strength also: "To destroy this monument," wired Leopold Stokowski, "would be eloquent testimony for the accusation leveled at Americans that we have little regard for the heritage that is rooted in cultural values. This would be another example of the American love of the material of which we have been too often and correctly accused."

Discussion of ticket prices at New York concert halls was stimulated and the Committee noted that the masses of New Yorkers were being priced out of enjoying their culture—but that the continuance of Carnegie Hall could correct this. Also at this time Leonard Bernstein and the New York Philharmonic fell on bad days with the critics. The orchestra was berated and its conductor accused of executing a preposterous *pas seul* on the podium. Thus, when the Committee's press releases spoke of a new professional symphony orchestra which might reside in Carnegie Hall when the Philharmonic moved into Lincoln Center, many important heads nodded approvingly. (This might be called the "Leopold Damrosch bogey" in New York.)

Meanwhile, the Simon management went ahead with its own plans, X-ing all windows with white paint and serving tenants with eviction notices dated March 31, 1960. The American National Theatre and Academy rented the Hall for a May 20 "Farewell to Carnegie Hall." Oddly enough, its roster of advisers for the program—Fritz Kreisler, Pablo Casals, Mrs. Eleanor Roosevelt, Stokowski, and ANTA Board Chairman Robert W. Dowling—all contributed to Citizens Committee work which ultimately made the "Farewell" inappropriate.

The March 31, 1960, deadline spurred Senator Mitchell to action. He fed his bill, the Bard Act Amendment, into the hopper at Albany. Simultaneously an identical bill was filed by the city Democrats. Following last-minute pressure, the Albany legislators slipped both bills through on March 30, 1960, and sent them to the governor for his signature. For Mr. Rockefeller the situation was not simple. He could not ignore the justice of the legislation or the fact that it was sponsored by both parties. Yet, his family's Rockefeller Foundation had already invested millions in Lincoln Center and had, in fact, turned down a request for save-Carnegie money two months before. Lincoln Center must not be threatened—but Rockefeller also realized that historic Carnegie Hall could not be allowed to collapse into rubble. He signed the bills which permitted any city in the state of New York to acquire by condemnation any property "with special historical or esthetic interest or value." Carnegie Hall was ready for deliverance.

The next step for the Citizens Committee was to convince the city's Board of Estimate that it should act immediately under the terms of the new law. City officials had already been liberally "massaged" by celebrities by the time their decision was to be made. But just to be sure, the Citizens Committee drafted a telegram, circulated it among friends for signature, then sent it to Mayor Wagner on April 1, his day of decision, as a way of showing their support for him. "To destroy [Carnegie Hall] now for 'practical reasons' is an act of irresponsibility damaging to the United States and our prestige in the entire civilized world," the message read in part. (The telegram also included a typical Stern-ism: the Hall had to be saved "for the development of the musicians of tomorrow.") It was signed by Pablo Casals, Leonard Bernstein, Gregor Piatigorsky, Jascha Heifetz, Eugene Ormandy, Vladimir Horowitz, Erica Morini, George Szell, Marian Anderson, Fritz Kreisler, Bruno Walter, Eugene Istomin, Dimitri Mitropoulos, Mischa Elman, Charles Munch, Mieczyslaw Horszowski, and Isaac Stern.

There could be no delay. Tenants in the studios must be encouraged to stay on; the few who had left, to be brought back: income would be needed if all went well. But most important, the saving of the Hall had to be accomplished before the concert managers of the city made up their 1960–61 schedules and booked their attractions into other halls. The doubts of the Stern committee were quickly allayed by the managers themselves. On April 1, at a hurried meeting of the Independent Concert Managers Association, Herbert Barrett offered a ringing resolution in support of Carnegie Hall, its Citizens Committee, and all public officials of like mind. The resolution ended with a plea for everyone to work fast, so that the Hall would be ready for the fall openings. Otherwise, the resolution darkly predicted, "the New York public will be deprived of a large part of its traditional artistic enjoyment and many of our best artists of their usual professional activity." Among the apprehensive signers were Barrett, Colbert-LaBerge, Ludwig Lustig, Eastman Boomer, and other vigorous managements who thus gave the Carnegie Hall committee the promise of a solid rental base if the city did what it should.

And so the mayor moved. On April 28 the Board of Estimate authorized the city's Department of Real Estate to acquire the Hall from Simon. On May 16 the mayor formally created the nonprofit Carnegie Hall Corporation, which then leased the Hall from the city for thirty years at an annual rental of $366,000 for the first year, to be reduced by $6,640 each year thereafter. (The lease also contained cancellation clauses that allowed the Lincoln Center group to ask the city to end the experiment and close down the Hall should it be overly competitive with the Center. Those clauses are no longer operative.)

In the nineteenth-floor sitting room of the Stern apartment, by the French doors that look out onto Central Park (with a clear view of the Shakespeare amphitheater, another project given key support by the Kaplans and Rubinow), hangs an illuminated framed document which reads:

Although the experts failed and all the wisest found no way, ISAAC STERN, heeding the poet's plea—'Sweet sounds, oh, beautiful music, do not cease!'—at last succeeded. To him, to his clear vision and persistence, we owe the preservation of a heritage, Carnegie Hall. Inscribed in gratitude, The Municipal Art Society of New York, May 18, 1960.

After a new paint job and general face-lifting, the Hall reopened for a preview on Sunday evening, September 25, 1960, with the New York Philharmonic, Leonard Bernstein, Isaac Stern, and a gala invitation-only audience. Two days before, Stern had been concertizing on the shores of Lake Geneva, at Montreux, Switzerland. After that concert he boarded a plane for New York, arriving in time for a last-minute preopening board meeting. With very little sleep and much telephoning, Stern passed the few hours remaining before the concert in the Hall.

Stern performed the Beethoven "Violin Concerto" with such passion that evening that he broke a string. When it was over, and the audience rose to give him a well-deserved ovation, he clutched his violin and did what he had never done before: Stern cried onstage before the cheering audience, as his inner feelings vied with the tumult in the Hall itself.

It was a busy few days. The next day, Monday, Mayor Wagner officiated at the formal ribbon-cutting. Assisting him was the city's own Department of Sanitation Band arrayed on the Fifty-seventh Street sidewalk. Wagner, one of four honorary members of New York Musicians Local 802 and a former music student who had learned the violin in a Carnegie Hall studio, briefly took the baton and conducted the band during one of its festive selections. On Tuesday, Stern and the whole Committee were special guests at a large fund-raising luncheon on the lawn of the mayor's Gracie Square mansion. ("We are all proud of this world-renowned Hall and we want to increase its influence on the musical life of all New Yorkers," said the engraved invitations.) That evening, Stern and Bernstein repeated the Beethoven program to open officially the Hall's seventieth season. After more board meetings and some last-minute instructions to his wife, Stern enplaned for London, arriving there in time for rehearsals for a Thursday evening concert.

Of the original founders, only Mrs. Feit is gone. She was stricken by cancer of the spine in April, when victory was finally assured, but was bedridden during the victory itself. Mrs. Feit died in midsummer.

To the other members of the "hard core"—Stern, Kaplan, Rubinow, deSimone, Richmond, Riegelman—has been added an executive director, Mr. Julius Bloom, former director of the Brooklyn Academy of Music for two decades, who, through his professional affiliation with Rutgers University, has been ardent in the cause of making more and better opportunities available to young musicians seeking a meaningful first exposure. And back in his Fifty-sixth Street office, after a brief tour of duty at Lincoln Center, is Mr. John Totten, the house manager.

Although there are some new faces among the management, the function of the Hall hasn't changed at all. It still serves as a free stage for the people of New York—indeed, of the whole world—to command in the cause of art, science, philosophy, religion, or just plain fun. The more the Hall's personnel changes, the more the Hall itself stays the same. Its program is still at times almost unbelievable. Muhammad's Temple No. 7 (the so-called Black Muslims) perform "Trial: Day of Reckoning for the White Man"; the Church of Divine Unity has a Sunday morning service; Carmel Quinn, Ireland's darling, follows Giovanni Buitoni, the bass-voiced head of the spaghetti company; the orchestras of New York, Boston, Vienna, Berlin, Philadelphia, London, Cleveland, Toronto, and St. Louis tumble in and out of the Hall; the laughter for Shelley Berman,

Dick Gregory, Nichols and May, Mort Sahl, and Lenny Bruce echoes from balcony to parquet. For Carnegie Hall still boasts the most eclectic list of coming attractions of any public gathering place in America. Isaac Stern, president of the Carnegie Hall Corporation, says: "Carnegie has always reflected the pluralism of our society and there's no reason why it shouldn't continue to do so. In fact, it *must* do this. Where else could many people find a hall in which to express themselves? But this Hall always has been—and always must be—open."

To the argument that such chaotic programming—in the face of Lincoln Center's precise programs—will only reduce the reputation of Carnegie Hall to the level of a vaudeville house (as was feared in the old days, when the directors stopped calling it a "music hall"), the new corporation answers that it has a large debt to retire and that if the Hall is not busy for the next few years, it will go dark forever. Constant traffic at the box office is Carnegie's best mortgage insurance at this point. But the new directors continue from there:

"We must also provide a stage for young talent, the girls and boys who will be the Rubinsteins, Bernsteins, and Heifetzes of tomorrow. How do they get a start? They will get it here at Carnegie Hall."

Stern wants new works to be sponsored by the Carnegie Hall Corporation itself and would like to underwrite the appearances in New York's major auditorium of rarely heard—but deserving—groups from overseas, as well as from our own hinterlands. In the 165 studios—"The only such collection of youth-training studios in this or any other city," says Stern—open spaces would be created for choreographers to notate new ballets. New devices, such as closed-circuit television and video-taping equipment, could be called into play. Everywhere that Stern or Bloom turns in Carnegie Hall, a dream appears.

And this has been—and continues to be—a Hall of dreams: for New York, for the United States, for the world. Or rather, the realization of dreams: from the nervous debut of a new artist to the meticulous program of an old professional, Carnegie Hall is where wonderful things happen.

PORTRAIT OF CARNEGIE HALL

1 * A Hall Is Built

CARNEGIE HALL has been identified with the cultural aspirations of America for more than seven decades. And, like the nation it mirrors, Carnegie has no real beginning to its story; it was the result of many related events stretching back through time. But if one circumstance must be chosen, it is the confrontation of two ambitious German violinists in late-nineteenth-century New York: Theodore Thomas and Leopold Damrosch.

Thomas arrived here in 1845, a ten-year-old prodigy with enough stamina to tour the clapboard "lyceums" of Jacksonian America. As a member of several orchestras, he put in a grueling apprenticeship playing the circus-concerts (horses on stage, spouting fire hoses, sirens) that were popular then. However, noting the box-office strength of "serious" music, Thomas organized his own orchestra and crisscrossed the nation to offer—instead of *Night, or the Firemen's Quadrille* and *The Tower of Babel, or Language Confounded*—the works of Beethoven, Brahms, Mozart, Liszt, and of his friends Wagner and Anton Rubinstein. Later, pianist-composer Rubinstein and violinist-composer Henri Wieniawski joined Thomas in pioneer recital tours. Hence, during the 1870's, Theodore Thomas stood at the peak of national musical influence. In 1877–1878, he was guest conductor of the New York Philharmonic (he had been a violinist in that orchestra 23 years before). Then, in 1880, Thomas returned as resident conductor of the Philharmonic, filling out a busy schedule by also conducting his own orchestra and the Brooklyn Symphony. The imprint of Theodore Thomas upon American musical history had now become clear and permanent.

In 1871 Leopold Damrosch arrived in New York with two sons, Walter Johannes and Frank Heino. Damrosch had abandoned medicine for a career in music, had left Germany for the opportunity of America. But the figure of Thomas was so dominant that both career and opportunity seemed beyond reach to the new arrival. Damrosch discussed the situation with Anton Rubinstein, who boldly suggested that Damrosch put together his own musical organization to equal Thomas's. In 1873, Damrosch's sixty-voice Oratorio Society of New York gave its first concert in the warerooms of the Knabe Piano Company. Five years later Damrosch was influential enough to found a new orchestra, the Symphony Society of New York, and to conduct its first concert in Steinway Hall. When Thomas assumed the podium of the Philharmonic in 1880, he posed a challenge to Damrosch for supremacy in New York.

However, the battlefield was uncomfortably small. New York, the omphalos of American music, had a number of small and medium halls sprinkled between Fourteenth and Fortieth streets: Steinway, Chickering, and Hardman halls (owned by piano-makers who doubled as impresarios), Mendelssohn Hall, the Academy of Music, and—the one large hall —the Metropolitan Opera House.

Competition for these halls grew fierce, especially for the big Opera House. In addition to the Damrosch and Thomas groups, there were the visiting orchestras of other cities and of Europe, plus the Metropolitan Opera company itself. New York—and particularly the Damrosch family—needed another big hall to consolidate leadership.

Leopold Damrosch died in 1885, willing his baton to twenty-three-year-old Walter. Handsome, ambitious as his formidable parent, a welcome guest in New York's wealthiest homes, Walter scouted about for a donor of a hall.

In April, 1887, Louise Whitfield took title to a mansion at 5 West Fifty-first Street, next to the Vanderbilts. It was a wedding gift from her husband, steel magnate Andrew Carnegie. A tiny man (130 pounds, size-five shoes), Andrew Carnegie had amassed a $15,000,000 fortune, which, as a philanthropist, he drew upon liberally to buy libraries, foundations, collections, churches, organs and schools. When

Louise and Andrew sailed on the *Fulda* for a honeymoon in Scotland, a young friend, Walter Damrosch, was also on board, heading for Germany to study with Hans von Bülow.

Carnegie invited the young man to visit his Dumfermline estate in Scotland. Walter accepted and the two men strengthened their bonds of friendship while driving about the grounds in a four-in-hand or sitting before the drawing-room fire. They discussed ideas of broad cultural significance—and also the specific problems of New York. Both agreed that the city needed another hall as big as the Opera House. And Andrew Carnegie's agreement amounted to $2,000,000, or nine-tenths the cost of such a hall.

Carnegie chose to bypass New York's tenderloin district (Twenty-fourth to Fortieth streets). Daringly he selected a plot of the old Cosine

a. Theodore Thomas

b. Anton Rubenstein Program

Leopold Damrosch and his son Walte

a. The Osborne, seen from empty Carnegie lot

farm on the edge of Goat Hill as the site of his "Music Hall." It was a leap into the suburbs. Nearby, sunning themselves on manicured lawns, were the leonine mansions of the Rockefellers and Vanderbilts, the Rogerses, Guggenheims, Huntingtons, and Depews. Diagonally across the dirt road was Stanford White's shallow-arched, veneer-inlaid, granite-walled Osborne Hotel, surrounded by low stables, some shacks, and an occasional saloon. In 1889, Osborne residents, Lillian Russell among them, looked out upon new excavation. The arts were coming uptown.

William Burnet Tuthill, an eclectic with a

b. Laying the cornerstone: Mrs. Carnegie under ladder at stone; Mr. Carnegie at center behind stone

large following, accepted the $35,000 commission to design the hall. (Like Hopper the builder and Herter the decorator, Tuthill collected much of his fee in Music Hall Company stock.) Tuthill's consultant was Richard Morris Hunt, founder and president of the American Institute of Architects, designer of the Tribune Tower and Statue of Liberty pedestal, champion of the elevator-skyscraper, and a man who felt that a touch of the Old Rome could not but enhance the New.

The Gilded Age was beginning to glow. Europe looked to America with less of its historic disdain or—at best—condescension. For New York, as well as for the nation, the nineteenth century was ending with a decade of ebullient splendor.

The Music Hall opened on May 5, 1891, with a five-day music festival, modeled on the Thomas festivals of Cincinnati and Chicago. Walter Damrosch, regent of music in New York (Thomas had withdrawn to establish the Chicago Symphony), planned a varied and exciting program. Highlights were the four appearances of Russia's leading composer, Pëtr Ilich Tchaikovsky.

Tchaikovsky was a happy choice in many respects. He had been a student of Anton

Fifty-seventh Street façade prior to formal opening

The "Music Hall"

MUSIC FESTIVAL

In Celebration of the Opening of

MUSIC HALL

CORNER 57TH STREET & 7TH AVENUE,

MAY 5, 6, 7, 8, and 9, 1891.

The Symphony Society Orchestra,

The Oratorio Society Chorus,

BOYS' CHOIR OF 100, (Wenzel Raboch, Choirmaster.)

AND THE FOLLOWING ARTISTS:

P. TSCHAIKOWSKY, the eminent Russian composer, who will conduct several of his own works.

FRAU ANTONIA MIELKE, Soprano,
MLLE. CLEMENTINE DE VERE, Soprano,
MRS. GERRIT SMITH, Soprano,
MRS. TH. J. TOEDT, Soprano,
MISS ANNA LUELLA KELLY, Soprano,
MRS. KOERT KRONOLD, Soprano,
FRAU MARIE RITTER-GOETZE, Contralto,
MRS. CARL ALVES, Contralto,
MRS. CLAPPER-MORRIS, Contralto.

SIGNOR ITALO CAMPININI, Tenor.
HERR ANDREAS DIPPEL, Tenor.
MR. THOMAS EBERT, Tenor,
HERR THEODOR REICHMANN, Baritone,
HERR EMIL FISCHER, Bass,
HERR CONRAD BEHRENS, Bass,
MR. ERICSON BUSHNELL, Bass,
FRL. ADELE AUS DER OHE, Pianist.
MR. FRANK L. SEALY, Organist

WALTER DAMROSCH,   -   CONDUCTOR.

THE MUSIC HALL COMPANY OF NEW YORK, Limited.

MORRIS RENO, President.

FREDERICK WILLIAM HOLLS, Secretary.   STEPHEN M. KNEVALS, Treasurer

DIRECTORS.

John W. Aitkin,	Frederick Wm. Holls,	Sherman W. Knevals,
Andrew Carnegie,	Wm. S. Hawk,	Morris Reno,
Walter J. Damrosch,	Stephen M. Knevals,	William B. Tuthill.

Opening poster

Rubinstein at the St. Petersburg Conservatory and of brother Nicholas Rubinstein at the Moscow Conservatory. His works, familiar to Americans, seemed to represent a union of the bravado and the innocence which characterized the America of 1891.

"A man of ample proportions," reported the New York *Herald*, "with gray hair, well built, of a pleasing appearance and about 60 years of age." (He was 51 two days later.) "He seemed rather nervous and answered the applause with a number of stiff little bows. . . ." The *Tribune*'s Henry Krehbiel noted that "his bearing was modest but unconstrained, his beat firm but undemonstrative."

On opening night the carriages were lined up for a quarter of a mile down Fifty-seventh Street. From them stepped "beautiful women in attractive gowns and men well-known in New York." Bishop Henry Codman Potter bustled in, wearing a shawl-roll dress coat and high-buttoned waistcoat. "All was quiet, dig-

Tchaikovsky

nified, soft, slow, and noiseless, as became the dedication of a great temple." In Box 1, overlooking the stage, was James G. Blaine, whose son-in-law, Walter Damrosch, was about to strike up "Old Hundred." Bishop Potter praised all who contributed to the Hall, lamented the absence of Leopold Damrosch, and singled out Andrew Carnegie for his "spirit of triumphant democracy." (Tchaikovsky later recalled, "A clergyman made a very long and wearisome speech in which he eulogized the founders of the hall, especially Carnegie.")

All 2,247 seats and 63 boxes were filled. "Tonight," one newspaper reported, "the most beautiful Music Hall in the world was consecrated to the loveliest of the arts. Possession of such a hall is in itself an incentive for culture."

In Box 33, center, first tier, sat Louise and Andrew Carnegie accepting the good wishes of 2,500 friends. Andrew was not always a wakeful patron of the arts. Tucked into a corner of the Box 33 foyer was an inviting couch, in case the business of the day should override the pleasure of the evening.

The festival progressed nicely, although Tchaikovsky, characteristically, began his American visit unhappily. He hadn't planned on being away from Moscow as long as proved necessary. Nevertheless, he warmed to America, was impressed with what little he saw here, and, indulging in his favorite perfumes and lavish clothes, ended by sadly enjoying himself. When he departed, he gave indications of wanting to return. However, two years and six months later, he drank a glass of unboiled water, contracted cholera, and died. Shortly before this, he had conducted the premiere of his *Sixth Symphony*, the "Pathétique," in St. Petersburg, and had thoughtfully mailed off the score to Walter Damrosch. Tchaikovsky's score—and the news of his death—arrived in New York together.

The career of Carnegie Hall was off to an auspicious start. But, more important, the course of American music—and much of its public life—was taking a new direction. The opening programs had a prophetic ring: the German influence would no longer dominate, but would share the stage with French and Russian influences for the next half-century.

PROGRAMMES.

TUESDAY EVENING, MAY 5TH, 1891.

"OLD HUNDRED."

ORATION.   DEDICATION OF THE HALL.
By the RIGHT REVEREND HENRY C. POTTER, D.D.

NATIONAL HYMN, "AMERICA."

OVERTURE, "LEONORE" No. III, ...   BEETHOVEN

INTERMISSION.

MARCHE SOLENNELLE   .   .   .   .   TSCHAIKOWSKY
Conducted by the Composer.

TE DEUM, ...   BERLIOZ
(First time in New York.)   For Tenor Solo, Triple Chorus and Orchestra.
SOLOIST—SIGNOR ITALO CAMPANINI.

WEDNESDAY EVENING, MAY 6TH, 1891.

ELIJAH," Oratorio for Soli, Chorus and Orchestra.   .   .   MENDELSSOHN
SOLOISTS
FRAU ANTONIA MIELKE, MISS ANNA L. KELLY, FRAU MARIE RITTER-GOETZE, MISS MAC PHERSON,
HERR ANDREAS DIPPEL, MR. THOMAS EBERT, HERR EMIL FISCHER, MR. BUSHNELL.

THURSDAY AFTERNOON, MAY 7TH, 1891.

OVERTURE TO "FIGARO,"   .   .   .   .   MOZART

GRAND FINALE, ACT II. "FIGARO,"   .   .   .   MOZART
FRAU MIELKE, MLLE. DE VERE, FRAU GOETZE, HERR DIPPEL HERR REICHMANN,
HERR FISCHER, HERR BEHRENS.

SUITE No. III, for Orchestra, ...   TSCHAIKOWSKY
Conducted by the Composer.

ARIA FROM L'ESCLARMONDE,   .   .   .   MASSENET
MLLE. DE VERE.

ARIA FROM "LE ROI DE LAHORE,"   .   .   .   MASSENET
HERR THEODOR REICHMANN.

PRELUDE AND FINALE FROM "TRISTAN AND ISOLDE,"   .   .   WAGNER

PROGRAMMES.

FRIDAY EVENING, MAY 8TH, 1891.

THE SEVEN WORDS OF OUR SAVIOUR, ...   HEINRICH SCHUETZ
(Seventeenth century.) (First time in America.)
For Soli, Chorus, String Orchestra and Organ.
SOLOISTS, { FRAU ANTONIA MIELKE,   FRAU MARIE RITTER-GOETZE,
          HERR ANDREAS DIPPEL,   HERR THEODOR REICHMANN,
                 MR. ERICSON BUSHNELL.

TWO A. CAPELLA CHORUSES: }
   a. PATER NOSTER,   (New. First time in America.)   TSCHAIKOWSKY
   b. LEGEND.
Conducted by the Composer.

SULAMITH.   .   .   .   .   .   .   LEOPOLD DAMROSCH
For Soli, Chorus and Orchestra.
Soloists, FRAU ANTONIA MIELKE,   HERR ANDREAS DIPPEL.

SATURDAY AFTERNOON, MAY 9TH, 1891.

FIFTH SYMPHONY, C MINOR, ...   BEETHOVEN

SONGS, { "TO SLEEP,"   .   .   .   WALTER DAMROSCH
        "SO SCHMERZLICH,"   .   .   .   TSCHAIKOWSKY

CONCERTO for Piano with Orchestra, B Flat Minor, Op. 23,   .   TSCHAIKOWSKY
     I.   Andante non troppo e molto maestoso.   Allegro con spirito.
     II.   Andantino Simplice.
     III.   Allegro con fuoco.
Piano, MISS ADELE AUS DER OHE.
Conducted by the Composer.

PRELUDE,   }
   FLOWER MAIDEN SCENE, ACT II,   } FROM PARSIFAL,   .   WAGNER
For six Solo Voices and Female Chorus.
MRS. GERRIT SMITH,   MRS. TOEDT.   MISS KELLY,   MRS. KOERT KRONOLD,
MRS. ALVES,   MRS. MORRIS.
Steinway & Sons' Piano used at this Concert.

SATURDAY EVENING, MAY 9TH.

"ISRAEL IN EGYPT" Oratorio, ...   HANDEL
For Soli, Double Chorus and Orchestra.
SOLOISTS:
MISS KELLY,   MRS. TOEDT,   MRS. ALVES,   HERR DIPPEL,
HERR FISCHER,   MR. BUSHNELL.

First Programs

a. The teens: People's Singing Classes and Choral Union on stage apron

b. The twenties: New York Symphony, Philadelphia Philharmonic together

c. The thirties: New York Philharmonic–Symphony Society

d. The forties: Bruno Walter conducting

e. The fifties: Leonard Bernstein conducting

20

2 * Symphony Orchestras

THE superiority of Carnegie Hall over all the auditoriums of New York was quickly recognized. The stage could accommodate more than the sixty-man orchestra of the day, though backstage was—and still is—uncomfortably cramped. In addition, by extending a stage apron to Row L (the eleven rows of seats were stored in a Fifty-sixth Street stable) it was possible to mass more than two hundred musicians onstage or to hold a grand ball, as the Union Boat Club, *Deutsche Kunstlerfest*, and others did. The Carnegie grand ballroom might still be used today, if the fire commissioner had not ruled by 1910 that the subapron would act as a giant flue in case of fire.

The décor of the Carnegie stage has reflected changing popular tastes. The old parchment lampshades were replaced by hidden banks of proscenium lights; the walls were given a disquieting Venetian treatment, and finally a restful neoclassical finish; the pipes of the massive $8,600 organ were discreetly hidden; neutral gray drapes eventually shrouded the side walls and concealed the broadcasting control booth; and a soft ivory tone was painted over all the surfaces, the most severe treatment so far, but one which evenly distributes the lighting and flatters those onstage.

But heroic proportions and rich appointments alone do not make a great hall; people are needed—people of genius, taste, and vision. From its opening night, Carnegie has had them. Among the first were Walter Damrosch and the Symphony Society. Dr. Damrosch is not remembered as a brilliant conductor; his

contribution, however, outlasted many of his colleagues': his was a continuing vision of the role of serious music in America, a vision he pursued with spirit and imagination in the Hall he helped to found.

The New York Philharmonic moved to Carnegie in 1892, when its home theater, the Opera House, was gutted by fire. The Philharmonic was then under the direction of Anton Seidl, a pupil of Wagner and von Bülow, and a romantic tempered by scholarship. Seidl maintained a heavy German and Austrian accent in his programs—with one exception: as much as 12 percent of his scores were from the pen of Antonin Dvorák, who was a visiting professor in New York at the time. Damrosch, favoring French, Russian, and native American composers, maintained a valiant competition with the Philharmonic, but seemed to run a close second in popularity. Although he proudly called his Symphony Society "the only permanent orchestra in New York," he had to suspend its activity between 1898 and 1903.

The competition between the New York orchestras was often of less interest to concertgoers than was the annual visit of the Boston Symphony Orchestra. The BSO played Carnegie first in 1893, but made the trip regularly from 1898 on. The classicist Wilhelm Gericke was then back as its musical director. Well subsidized by Henry Lee Higginson and fiercely proud of its historic sponsor-city, the BSO was built and rebuilt by a succession of brilliant conductors: Gericke; Arthur Nikisch, an in-

a. Anton Seidl

b. Karl Muck

c. Victor Herbert

tensely exciting Viennese sometimes recalled as "the first prima donna conductor"; and Karl Muck, who had no peer in matters Wagnerian.

Until World War I, the Carnegie podium was dominated by the finest graduates of German and Austrian conservatories. (Probably the only well known exception was American-born John Philip Sousa, a graduate of the United States Marine Band.) In addition, there were about eighty key opera houses in Germany and Austria which provided excellent training for young conductors; these houses were periodically raided by American boards of directors in search of next season's maestros. Of all such talent imported in those years, Gustav Mahler was probably the most important.

Mahler had been conductor of the Hamburg Opera (his assistant there: eighteen-year-old Bruno Walter), of the Budapest Royal Opera, then director of the Vienna Imperial Opera. In 1907 he was invited to lead the Metropolitan. The following year Mahler was appointed to direct a reorganized Philharmonic at Carnegie Hall. He took over with the blessings of Joseph Pulitzer, Andrew Carnegie, J. P. Morgan, and other friends of the orchestra. Mahler extended the orchestra's season, enriched it with a Beethoven cycle and other special events, added a tour, and, above all, infused it with his own highly charged, highly controversial personality.

But he was more than the Philharmonic committeewomen could abide. They were bewildered by his own works; Mahler finished his *Symphony of a Thousand* while in New York, and its grandiose canvas repelled the ladies. Like Nikisch (who enjoyed more tolerance in Boston), Mahler freely edited the works of other composers (except Wagner) if he felt it worthwhile—adding kettledrums to Beethoven's *Sixth Symphony* or doubling the flutes in Mozart's *Symphony No. 40*—which further enraged the committeewomen. He began early in his brief (1908–1911) tenure to feel their power. He grew to hate them and their pretentious city. Subscription lists dwindled; orchestra morale slipped. In the mornings, preparing to go to rehearsal, Mahler felt "like an old steer making up his mind to go to the slaughterhouse." Eventually he overtaxed his heart: On February 21, 1911, during the forty-seventh concert of his third season, Mahler collapsed and was rushed to Paris for treatment. He died three months later in Vienna.

Sharing a crowded Carnegie calendar with the great city orchestras were a number of smaller organizations which made noteworthy contributions to American musical history. Some were the properties of their conductors, such as the Hermann Hans Wetzler Orchestra; others were founded on a broader base, such as the Russian Symphony Orchestra. The Russian Symphony, organized by Modest and Jacob Altschuler, introduced the works of Borodin, Scriabin, Rimsky-Korsakov, and Glazunov to Carnegie audiences, and brought such sensational soloists as Josef Lhevinne and Mischa Elman to America's attention. With his group of hardy missionaries, including the violin prodigy Fredric Fradkin as concertmaster,

a. Fritz Busch

b. John Philip Sousa

Modest Altschuler also barnstormed the nation, playing these exotic new East European scores.

The Russian Symphony thus set a new standard in vigor as well. The average season for a symphony orchestra was rather spare: the Philharmonic, for example, had but six annual concerts in the 1880's. William Steinway used this as a point in arguing against the building of Carnegie Hall. "They [the six concerts] are not given at a loss because they are supported by subscription. But increase the number of these high-class [*sic*] concerts to twelve and financial disaster would be certain. The public can only stand a certain amount of this sort of music." And in those balmy pre-Local 802 days the orchestra member earned seven dollars a concert, plus an extra two dollars per rehearsal. Of course, the times have changed. Today, as many as forty events (not counting rehearsals) take place each week in Carnegie's various halls—and most of them are "high-class concerts." The Philharmonic itself gave more than 120 concerts during its last (1961–1962)

c. Gustav Mahler

season there. And today's musician is guaranteed $200 a week, plus fringe benefits, for a minimum 42-week season.

The Altschulers were also ahead of their time in their consistent advocacy of French and Russian music. A swing away from German influence was in motion prior to World War I, but the events of 1914 gave it additional momentum. After America entered the war in 1917, German conductors and composers were *personae non gratae* in many American halls. The Boston Symphony's Karl Muck was badgered for not playing "The Star-Spangled Banner" (actually Colonel Higginson's decision), and was finally interned for reasons never made public. The Cincinnati's Ernst Kunwald played the national anthem, but did not properly acknowledge the applause which followed; he also was imprisoned and deported for undisclosed reasons. Modern German and Austrian composers were discreetly left out of programs. Even performers felt the pressure: Fritz Kreisler, veteran of the Austrian Army but in the States while the fighting was still in progress, voluntarily withdrew from all engagements in 1918, losing a reported $85,000 in fees.

As German influence declined, Franco-Russian influence increased. Tchaikovsky dominated the repertoire—as much as 20 percent in some orchestras. Eugène Ysaÿe, the Belgian violin virtuoso, took over the Cincinnati; Henri Rabaud (1918) and Pierre Monteux (1919) assumed control of the Boston Sym-

a. Willem Mengelberg

b. Edwin Franko Goldman

c. Serge Koussevitsky

d. Pierre Monteux

e. Albert Stoessel

phony. Debussy, D'Indy, Franck, and Stravinsky were given wider hearings. The Cortot-Thibaud-Casals trio, Sergei Rachmaninoff, and Ossip Gabrilowitsch were among the new wave of the twenties.

The upheaval in the music world during that decade brought to Carnegie Hall perhaps no greater genius than a Parma-trained cellist, conductor at La Scala and the Metropolitan, an Italian nationalist who despised Mussolini: Arturo Toscanini. On January 14, 1926, Toscanini began his association with the Philharmonic, the orchestra's first Italian conductor. A champion of Italian music, he gave the premiere of Respighi's *Pines of Rome* that evening (oddly enough there was no Beethoven on the Maestro's first program). The following month he was off to La Scala, the first of many shuttlings between Milan and New York. When in New York he quarreled, sulked, cursed, and thoroughly dispelled the Coolidge euphoria that often crept into Carnegie precincts. Sharing duties with Willem Mengelberg, for whom he had little respect, Toscanini was nevertheless principally responsible for raising the New York orchestra to the same heights of leadership then occupied by Koussevitzky's Boston and Stokowski's Philadelphia. Though he was slow in promoting American composers, Toscanini did offer new works by European contemporaries (Honegger's *Pastoral d'été*, Ravel's *Bolero*, Shostakovich's *First Symphony*), and a string of Bach compositions, many arranged by Toscanini's friend Ottorino Respighi. Beethoven and Wagner, his favorites, were generously represented. In 1928, when the Symphony Society and the Philharmonic were at last merged, ending a forty-year competition, Toscanini, whose presence largely influenced the merger, was appointed director. Later, he opposed a suggested merger of the Philharmonic with the Metropolitan.

On April 29, 1936, Toscanini ended his sojourn with the Philharmonic with a Beethoven-Wagner concert. Characteristically, Toscanini had all proceeds divided among the orchestra, the Musicians' Emergency Fund, and the staffs of the Philharmonic-Symphony Society and Carnegie Hall. A year later, however, he was in Studio 8H, Radio City, heading his own

Arturo Toscanini

(Above) At rehearsal, (Below) checking the score and (Right) during a performance

orchestra, the NBC Symphony. He made weekly broadcasts of great music to millions of Americans, and so realized the grand dream of Theodore Thomas. Eventually, Studio 8H proved too confining and Toscanini was back at Carnegie Hall for his weekend broadcasts. His NBC schedule held, with few breaks, for seventeen years. Toward the end Toscanini grew more short-tempered, vilified musicians and guests, broke batons and music stands without number; yet he maintained his orchestra at the summit. Then, during the April 3, 1954, dress rehearsal, Toscanini lost all patience and reason. Flinging a *"Mi vergogno di loro!"* ("I am ashamed of you!") at the orchestra, he stalked offstage. That evening he announced his retirement. The following day's broadcast—an all-Wagner program—was the Maestro's farewell.

In the years between the wars, Carnegie Hall was the nation's showcase for great symphonic and choral music: Gabrilowitsch and the Detroit Symphony, Frederick Stock and the Chicago, Fritz Reiner and the Cincinnati, Albert Coates and the Rochester; Albert Stoessel and the Oratorio Society (performing the Bach *B Minor Mass* complete for the first time, Easter, 1928); the conductorless American Symphonic ensemble; the Westminster Choir,

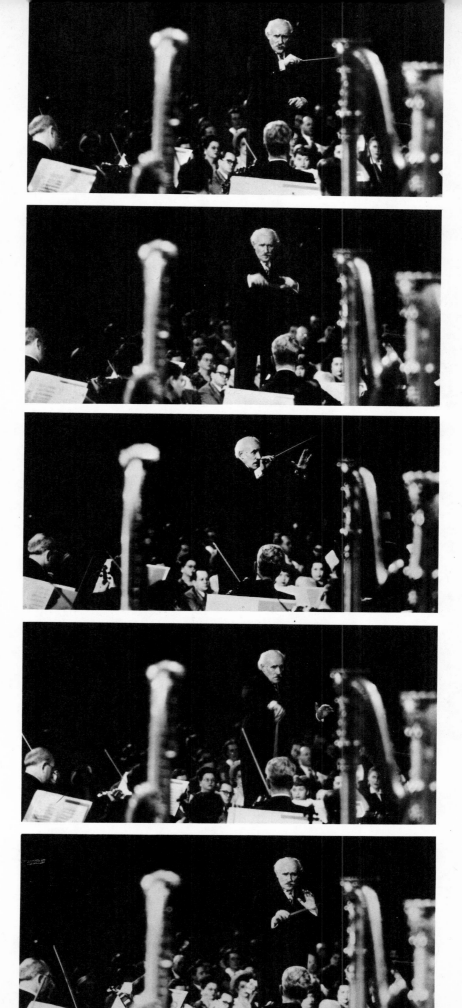

a. André Kostelanetz

b. Charles Munch

e. Fritz Reiner

d. Eugene Ormandy

c. Artur Rodzinski

The musicians' room backstage

Schola Cantorum, Paulist Choristers, the Dessoff Choir, and many adult and children's choirs from abroad. Josef Stransky brought an "era of good feeling" to the Philharmonic (with the help of a Pulitzer bequest). However, for the critics and the audience faithful, Carnegie was principally the setting for a great rivalry between two non–New York orchestras: Serge Koussevitzky's Boston and Leopold Stokowski's Philadelphia.

Koussevitzky was given the baton of the BSO in 1924, arriving in November of that year in Carnegie Hall. He was already fifty years old and had built an excellent record in Europe as a double-bass virtuoso and a conductor. In some ways he did for Czarist and Revolutionary Russia what Thomas had done for America: he organized symphony orchestras, published serious music for other orchestras to play, and traveled the waterways of the sprawling motherland to bring great music to villages hitherto unaware of its beauties. He was given official status by the Bolsheviks, but fled in disillusionment to Paris in 1920. There, again like Thomas, he organized his own orchestra around a repertoire of new French and Russian music. And at fifty his energy was undiminished and his devotion to new music was unwavering.

Although he began slowly, giving a puzzling preference to the works of Scriabin, in ensuing seasons he allowed his musical interests to roam across the broad American frontier as well as across the Continent. Through the Koussevitzky Music Foundation, established in 1942, new music came from the pens of Britten, Milhaud, Villa-Lobos, Schoenberg, Stravinsky, and especially Copland, who was consistently championed by the Boston Symphony. Koussevitzky explored new music without raising the hackles of his sponsors, a good indication of the man's warmth and charm. He was deeply loved by his Boston and New York audiences. (Henry Levinger, musicologist and close friend, remembers the throngs of elegantly gowned women who would crowd into the Carnegie Green Room after a concert, giving rise to the pun, Serge "Kissevoutzky.") He left the Boston to Charles Munch in 1951, but was to return again to the Carnegie stage as conductor of the new Israel Philharmonic during its 1955 tour here—a tour assisted by Koussevitzky as a belated gesture toward his Jewish parentage.

The second great non–New York orchestra, the Philadelphia, was led by a brash, publicity-conscious Londoner named Leopold Stokowski. An organist by training, Stokowski left the keyboards of New York's St. Bartholomew's to direct the creaking Cincinnati Symphony in 1909. A Bach scholar, he began conventionally enough—even used a baton at the time—but was not above scolding an inattentive audience, quarreling with his board, or programming new American music. His was a brief three-year romance between the proper German style of Van der Strucken and the unfortunate Kunwald.

In 1912, Stokowski took over the Philadelphia and developed it—and himself—into major musical forces. An enthusiast for sound, Stokowski shuffled his musicians' seating, introduced the Thereminvox and Clavilux (then thankfully forgot about them), and during Carnegie visits gave such programs as this one of January 6, 1932: *Two Cuban Dances*, by A. G. Caturla ("furious, tonally bifurcated music," reported *Times* critic Olin Downes); Efrem Zimbalist's *Daphnis and Chloe;* Milhaud's *Concerto for Percussion Instruments*, including a *tambourin de Provence* and a metal block; the premiere of Stravinsky's *Violin Concerto;* Alexander Mossolov's *Soviet Iron Foundry*, featuring steel plates and standing trumpets; ending with the Mussorgsky-Ravel *Pictures at an Exhibition*. (Such percussive programming was not rare in the twenties and thirties. On April 10, 1927, Eugene Goossens gave the American premiere of George Antheil's *Ballet mécanique* in Carnegie Hall. Its "orchestration" included auto horns, anvils, assorted bells, jangling engines, and several player-pianos. The audience howled in pain; a man in the first row got up and waved a white handkerchief in surrender; the reviews next day were barely printable.)

Stokowski left the Philadelphia in 1936, shared the NBC Symphony with Toscanini; moved restlessly about film and radio studios composing and conducting for the new media, organized the All-American Youth Orchestra, and then settled briefly as coproprietor of the Philharmonic (with Mitropoulos). The Houston Symphony beckoned, as did the NBC Symphony, reorganized (after Toscanini's departure) in Carnegie Studio 1101. Indefatigable at the age of eighty-two, Stokowski returned to Carnegie Hall in October, 1962, to lead his new American Symphony Orchestra (among its board members: Mrs. John F. Kennedy), which makes Carnegie Hall its home base.

Another Londoner will be remembered as a great Carnegie conductor: Sir Thomas Beecham. With the help of the Beecham's Pills treasury (". . . two for man and one for child . . ."), Sir Thomas founded—in the grand tradition of Jullien, Thomas, and Koussevitzky—the Beecham Symphony of London in 1908 and later the Beecham Opera. He was, however, no dilettante (despite poor training); his American debut at Carnegie Hall, January 12, 1928, was eagerly awaited.

He mounted the podium that evening "groomed and mundane . . . surveyed the audience and the hall with deliberate interest while the audience surveyed him. . . ." On the program that evening was Vladimir Horowitz, a twenty-three-year-old Russian virtuoso making his debut, also. It was not a happy coincidence. Beecham and Horowitz plunged into

Sir Thomas Beecham

Dimitri Mitropoulos

Tchaikovsky's *Concerto in B Flat Minor* and proceeded at different tempi until the final bar. The audience registered wild approval for Horowitz, whose stamina and technique were especially praiseworthy that evening. But Sir Thomas regained his composure and the favor of all for the remainder of the program. At the conclusion, he walked carefully offstage and into the Green Room—where he attended to his snapped suspenders!

On March 8, 1961, shortly before his eighty-second birthday, Sir Thomas died in London, and the world lost an exceptionally versatile conductor (opera, ballet, as well as symphony orchestras), and one of its most genial citizens. To the Carnegie audience, the death of Sir Thomas was the second of three in the space of sixteen months which were deeply mourned. The first was the passing of Dimitri Mitropoulos on November 2, 1960, at the comparatively young age of sixty-four. From his native Athens, Mitropoulos had moved about Europe achieving distinction not only as a pianist but as a conductor as well. In Berlin he was acclaimed for an appearance in both capacities. Koussevitzky, ever aware of new talent here and abroad, invited Mitropoulos to appear with the BSO in 1936. The Minneapolis Symphony —after an abrupt resignation by its conductor Eugene Ormandy—joined in the invitation, had Mitropoulos come to Minneapolis as a guest conductor, and then signed him on in

Leopold Stokowski

1937. For a man of Mitropoulos' energy and devotion, it was an excellent appointment. The Minneapolis had a strong financial base since its 1903 inception, when Elbert Carpenter, the Lumber King, founded it and installed his friend, the gifted Emil Oberhoffer, as its first conductor. Oberhoffer, like Thomas and the Altschulers, took his orchestra on innumerable trips to small towns to spread the gospel of good music. When Mitropoulos arrived as its fourth conductor, the Minneapolis was a well disciplined, fine-sounding instrument. He imparted to it what it had never had, however: intense feelings, curiosity, and daring. Endowed with an amazing memory and a strong physique (his hobby was mountaineering), Mitropoulos sought out whatever challenges new or old music would offer and joined with his friend Koussevitzky in championing the works of Copland, Barber, Bloch, and other new composers.

Mitropoulos left the Minneapolis in 1949 to direct the New York Philharmonic. In 1957–1958 he was assisted by his young friend and pupil, Leonard Bernstein, to whom he relinquished the baton the following year. Mitropolous moved on into opera, and it was at La Scala, during a rehearsal of Mahler's *Third Symphony,* that his heart suddenly stopped.

A measure of the love he had earned while in New York might be implied by the special "Tribute to Dimitri Mitropoulos," held in Carnegie Hall on March 5, 1961. Van Cliburn played Prokofieff's *Third Piano Concerto* and conducted the Symphony of the Air from the bench. A transparent piano lid gave him full view of the orchestra. This was precisely what Mitropoulos himself had done in 1953 with the Philharmonic; Cliburn's gesture recalled the genius of the dead maestro. A few weeks later, on April 1st, Bernstein and the Philharmonic performed Mahler's *Third,* sensitive to every passage as Mitropoulos himself would have been. Typical also was the fact that proceeds of both concerts went to funds to aid musicians, a cause with which Dimitri Mitropoulos had been identified all his life.

Cliburn's appearance as a Carnegie conductor was of some interest, since it was known in musical circles that he was studying under a master of the art, Bruno Walter. A pupil and friend of Gustav Mahler, Walter was unlike nearly every other conductor to appear in the

Hall. He was a deeply sensitive, modest man with none of the affectations that produced good "copy" in newspapers or magazines. He was seen in Carnegie first in 1923 with the old New York Symphony and returned for two more seasons as a guest. In 1932, after European successes in opera as well, Walter came back to the New York Philharmonic as a guest and several times thereafter, a restrained and thoughtful contrast to the fiery resident, Arturo Toscanini. Walter preferred Europe, but was dogged by the Nazis from city to city —Leipzig, Vienna, Paris—finally settling in America in 1941 as the Metropolitan's resident director. (His *Fidelio* earned him thirteen curtain calls.)

Walter was no stranger to the Philharmonic, however; indeed, one of the most important musical events of the war years was his uncut version of Bach's *Passion According to St. Matthew* in 1943 and repeated for several years after that. Walter was also chosen to direct the Philharmonic in 1947. His influence was sorely needed, for the orchestra had not been well cared for after Toscanini left. John Barbirolli, a thirty-seven-year-old British conductor and cellist, was invited to take over, at Toscanini's suggestion. Barbirolli was given full control of a disappointed orchestra and

—in the midst of the Great Depression—Sir John had to make the orchestra pay its own way. Although he had had wide experience (had even, in the grand tradition, organized his own Barbirolli Orchestra in England), the New York situation was beyond his power to correct. When Barbirolli left in 1941, escaping to the London blitz, the Philharmonic board called in Artur Rodzinski to do the kind of rebuilding job he had done for the Los Angeles and the Cleveland Symphonies. Rodzinski's first act was to fire fourteen men, including six first-desk players. His iron hand continued to lie heavy until the 1946-1947 season, when another round of firings touched off a small war and he resigned in fury. This was when Bruno Walter—a scholar and gentleman—took over and brought the orchestra back to the serious business of symphonic music. (Virgil Thomson summed it up by saying "Walter *musiziert*—Walter makes music.") When he left in 1949, the orchestra was in shape to accept and follow the dynamic lead of Mitropoulos. Among the most grieved at the news of Walter's death, February 17, 1962, were the 110 men and women of the New York Philharmonic, to whom Bruno Walter had given a new dignity and purpose when they needed them most.

Bruno Walter

Throughout the years the musicians in the symphony orchestras at Carnegie have made, and rarely tarnished, the reputations of dozens of conductors. Late to unionize, these musicians are highly individual, though they produce a community of sound. A spirit of genial chaos has always prevailed in the musicians' barrackslike locker room that faces Fifty-sixth Street. The fortunes of music are taken in stride; yet this talented group should get at least part credit for a performance that brought a new personality into the inner circle of great conductors.

On November 14, 1943, Assistant Conductor Leonard Bernstein walked to the Carnegie podium. Rodzinski, the orchestra's permanent conductor, was on leave; Bruno Walter was to have been guest conductor. Walter was ill that morning; he notified the twenty-five-year-old assistant that the program was now in his hands.

Bernstein spent the day with his scores: Schumann's *Manfred Overture,* Strauss's *Don Quixote,* and the premiere of Miklós Rózsa's *Theme, Variations, and Finale.* Dr. Walter had rehearsed the orchestra according to his own interpretations; but the performance was now in the hands of a young stranger.

A Carnegie audience of 2,500 and a radio audience of several million sighed at the appearance of the substitute, who was known to only a few. He wore a plain business suit, carried no batons. But the program was hardly under way before audience courtesy turned to enthusiasm. The interpretations were clearly not Walter's, yet they were neither shallow nor commonplace. It was a vibrant, sensitive job. Bernstein was recalled for many bows. The following day, newspapers carried his story on the front pages; a deluge of fan mail arrived. And so had Leonard Bernstein.

Bernstein began his career as a pianist, as did his friend and sponsor Dimitri Mitropoulos. He is still remembered at Harvard for his improvisations during showings of old silent films. While there he studied with Walter Piston and Edward Burlingame Hill. He had further guidance at the Curtis Institute under Fritz Reiner, and was given shape and substance by Serge Koussevitzky at Tanglewood.

a. Mr. Bernstein in 1943

b. Three generations at Carnegie Hall: Dr. Walter Damrosch, Paul Whiteman, Leonard Bernstein

Rehearsing in mufti; performing in tails

Rodzinski tutored him at Carnegie Hall. Bernstein grew in an awesomely brief time into a leading musical force. Taxiing between Carnegie and Broadway, he has added two symphonies *(Jeremiah, The Age of Anxiety),* two ballets *(Fancy Free* and one based on *Anxiety),* a one-act opera *(Trouble in Tahiti),* four musicals *(On the Town, Wonderful Town, Candide, West Side Story),* incidental theater music (the Mary Martin *Peter Pan),* and countless exciting piano performances to the landscape of American music.

Taking charge of the Philharmonic in 1958, Bernstein cozened it and his audience into a new *esprit.* Subscription lists were in fact waiting lists. The concept of the festival was revived as an educational device: a Mahler Festival, Festival of Theater Music, Keys to

the Twentieth Century, lending continuity to the full season. Balancing the classics were pieces by modern composers, including a *Concerto for Kazoo* and another for orchestra and tape recorder. An astonishing longhair success on close-shorn television, Bernstein expanded the Carnegie capacity to a home viewing audience of over thirty million.

The contrast between the Old-World Classicism of Theodore Thomas and the New-World romanticism of Leonard Bernstein has been played—sometimes even fought—out on the stage of Carnegie Hall. During every performance the watching presence of history has been felt more deeply here than in any other American auditorium. Its unique world position (mail addressed simply "Carnegie Hall, U.S.A." is promptly delivered) adds a piquancy to each program, an incentive for excellence that no other hall exerts so consistently—and with such brilliant results—upon conductors and musicians. And the knowledge that every note played can be heard by every listener in the Hall, thanks to its remarkable acoustics, is both reassuring and humbling.

For the composer a Carnegie performance of his work is a fair and generous test. After Tchaikovsky, the first composer so honored was Antonín Dvorák, whose *First Symphony,* presented on December 16, 1892, was also the Philharmonic's first premiere program in Carnegie Hall. Anton Seidl had the honor of introducing also Dvorák's *Fifth Symphony,* "From the New World," a year-less-a-day later. Claude Debussy, whose impressionism influenced a generation of American composers, was first performed in New York by the Boston Symphony, March 21, 1907, with the premiere here of *La Mer.* "The Sea [*sic*] is persistently ugly," said the *Times* the next day. "There is more barnyard cackle in it than anything else." "The dreariest kind of rubbish," said the *Post.* "A painted mud-puddle," scoffed the *Sun. Fountains of Rome,* by Ottorino Respighi, was introduced by Josef Stransky in 1919. Respighi himself arrived in the Hall on December 31, 1925, as soloist in the world premiere of his *Concerto for Piano in the Mixolydian Mode. Pines of Rome* was introduced at Toscanini's first Carnegie concert

a. Anton Dvorák

b. Claude Debussy

c. Ottorino Respighi

d. Richard Strauss

Whiteman and Damrosch

a month later. As soloist, conductor, and Bach transcriber, Respighi was a frequent Carnegie guest. The music of Richard Strauss was first heard in Carnegie in 1900 (a performance of *Ein Heldenleben*). Strauss himself arrived in 1904 as guest of the Hermann Hans Wetzler Orchestra and led the Philharmonic in his own works during that season also. "An elegant seigneur of uncommonly tall and slender figure . . . a giant of a man" is a contemporary description of Strauss. In 1921, Strauss was back for another American tour, beginning with a Carnegie appearance.

This parade of new music stimulated American composers. Something of a breakthrough came in the mid-twenties with the emergence of George Gershwin, a Tin Pan Alley songsmith ("Lady Be Good," "Swanee," five *Scandals* for George White), who was developing into a serious composer. Gershwin appeared in Aeolian Hall in 1923 to accompany Eva Gauthier, and in February, 1924, to play *Rhapsody in Blue* on a Paul Whiteman program called "Experiment in Modern Music." (Ferde Grofé, Whiteman's arranger and a composer also, orchestrated the *Rhapsody*.) Gershwin repeated his performance in Carnegie in April in a curious program that included "Dixie Land One Step" and "Japanese Sandman." Said the *Herald Tribune*'s Lawrence Gilman: "Weep over the lifelessness of the melody and harmony, so derivative, so stale, so inexpressive!" At Whiteman's suggestion, Walter Damrosch convinced Symphony Society president Harry Harkness Flagler to

commission Gershwin to write a serious piece for the orchestra. The young composer retired to Ernest Hutcheson's country home, spent the summer and fall of 1925 on his *Piano Concerto in F*, finished the orchestration himself on November 10th. Then, on December 3, 1925, Walter Damrosch conducted the world premiere of the *Concerto* with Gershwin at the piano. Still, the critics, except for praise-singing Samuel Chotzinoff, were unimpressed, detected too much Debussy in the score. It might be noted that earlier critics saw too much Dvořák (who had taught Gershwin's own teacher, Rubin Goldmark) in the more idiomatic *Rhapsody*. Damrosch defended Gershwin, said he lifted "Lady Jazz . . . to a level that would enable her to be received as a respectable member in musical circles." Three weeks later, Paul Whiteman concertized Grofé's *Mississippi Suite* and Gershwin's one-act opera *Blue Monday*, featuring Blossom Seeley, Jack McGowan, and Benny Fields, at Carnegie Hall. In 1928 Damrosch led the newly merged Philharmonic-Symphony Society in the world premiere of Gershwin's symphonic poem, *An American in Paris*. "Thumped the lid off in Carnegie Hall . . . an amusing occasion," was how Oscar Thompson of the *Post* dismissed it. "Nauseous claptrap . . . long-winded and inane," scowled Herbert Peyser of the *Telegram*.

For many years American music was principally confined to private performances and hasty matinees. Dudley Buck, John Knowles Paine, Ethelbert Nevin, Edward MacDowell, and a handful more were an early "advance

a. Ferde Grofé

b. George Gershwin

Igor Stravinsky

wave." A few others, like Henry Gilbert, experimented with Indian and Negro themes, but with small success. Later, John Alden Carpenter pursued a special brand of Midwestern whimsy; "Out is wonderful!" say the program notes to his *Adventures in a Perambulator*. And Charles Ives quietly ticked off the future in his Danbury, Connecticut, parlor.

Meanwhile, Modest Altschuler, with his Russophilic intuition, presented Stravinsky scores for the first time in Carnegie: *Fireworks* (in 1910) and *The Faun and the Shepherdess* (in 1918). This was the catalyst. In 1922 Stokowski revived *Fireworks* with a performance that convinced other directors to place at least one Stravinsky piece in every season series thereafter. Yet the really memorable stir took place in February, 1924, when *The Rite of Spring* was given by the Boston Symphony under Pierre Monteux, the same conductor who first presented the ballet (and touched off a riot) in Paris eleven years earlier. "After the first part of the score had come to an end," reported Olin Downes, "there were a few hisses—whether in indignation or to suppress premature applause was not easy to tell." At the conclusion the applause was "long and loud." Exactly a year later, Stravinsky, then forty-three, visited the United States. On February 6th he performed an undistinguished piano concerto that caused some laughter on the parquet.

The cause of Stravinsky was nevertheless stoutly advanced by the Boston Symphony under Koussevitsky and by the Philadelphia under Stokowski. Toscanini was unimpressed; Barbirolli was uncommitted. With the coming of Rodzinski, a perennial storm center, the Philharmonic revived its Stravinsky repertoire. The composer has even appeared with the orchestra and Bernstein on television.

Avant-garde music has been introduced at other halls besides Carnegie. Stravinsky's chamber and ballet pieces were first heard in other cities. Giving an unusual performance in Carnegie, a large and expensive auditorium, is more likely to be a sign of acceptance than of contrariety. In 1919, for example, futurist Edgard Varèse introduced his New Symphony

Orchestra at Carnegie, but had to abandon the Hall for smaller halls and theaters. (Varèse had barely arrived here after World War I when he packed the Philharmonic, the Symphony Society, and a chorus of six hundred into the old Sixth Avenue Hippodrome for a complete performance of Berlioz's *Requiem*.) The smaller, 299-seat Recital Hall has been a favorite of modernists, except that (until recently) New York's critics rarely bothered to drop in. Nevertheless, two forces, with momentum built up over seventy years, have kept Carnegie Hall as the center of musical progress. The first is its status as a special kind of building; the second is the Carnegie audience itself. While orchestras in other cities can cater to their own publics, an orchestra at Carnegie plays for an audience which reaches far beyond Manhattan. Radio and television broadcasts (averaging one a week) further dramatized Carnegie as *the* national hall of music. Among

a. Stravinsky

b. Ernest Ansermet, Franco Autori and Stravinsky

c. From left: Samuel Barber, Stravinsky, Lukas Foss, Aaron Copland and Roger Sessions

d. Autori, Stravinsky and Robert Craft on Fifty-sixth Street

a. Darius Milhaud

b. Paul Hindemith

the best-selling recordings of recent years have been those of actual Carnegie performances (see "A Carnegie Discography" at the end of this book). Hence, those who appear in the hall—whether it's the Moscow State Symphony or the Gramercy Chamber Ensemble—are aware of its eminence and feel constrained from offering anything run-of-the-mill. While this ensures interest and sometimes brilliance —disaster can also result.

Dimitri Mitropoulos and the Philharmonic spent an uncomfortable few minutes on December 18, 1929; they gave the first performance of Anton von Webern's *Symphony for Chamber Orchestra,* a work commissioned by the League of Composers, child of Varèse's International Composers Guild. The audience began by giggling and ended by laughing and snorting. Early in this ten-minute work men got up and retired to the lobby for a smoke and a smile. "Yells of laughter that came from all over the hall," reported Downes, "nearly drowned the sounds of Webern's simpering orchestra." Similarly, on March 31, 1960, Leonard Bernstein and the Philharmonic, divided into groups and scattered among the boxes and in the balcony, gave Henry Brant's highly cerebral *Antiphony One;* Pierre Boulez's *Improvisation sur Mallarmé 1* for soprano, harp, and assorted percussion; and *Concerted*

Piece for Tape Recorder and Orchestra by Otto Luening and Vladimir Ussachevsky, the latter operating the tape machine. Mr. Bernstein artfully rebuilt his demolished audience with a surprise rendition of Ravel's *La Valse,* an old crowd-pleaser.

One of the prime influences of the modern movement has been Nadia Boulanger. In 1962, the last year of the Philharmonic in Carnegie Hall, Mme. Boulanger came to New York to celebrate her seventy-fifth birthday with many of her friends and former students. She gave two concerts—February 15th and 18th —and became the first woman to conduct a full program with the Philharmonic. (The only other woman to conduct the Philharmonic at all was Rosalyn Tureck who, in 1958, led the Bach portion of the program from the keyboard.) Mme. Boulanger had been in the Hall once before: in 1939 she alternated between the podium and a piano and organ. During her earlier engagement she played an organ piece written by her sister Lili, a composer of great promise who died young. In 1962, she also included an orchestra piece by Lili, as well as *Requiem Mass* by composer-organist Gabriel Fauré (who taught Mme. Boulanger) and *A Solemn Music* by Virgil Thomson (whom Mme. Boulanger taught). From one viewpoint, her appearance in this, the final year of Carne-

a. Carlos Chavez

b. Dmitri Shostakovich

gie Hall as New York's supreme center of music, was especially fitting. Her life spanned the life of Carnegie Hall as well as the musical tastes of the seven decades. With her from Fauré's studio had come Maurice Ravel, Jean Roger-Ducasse, and Georges Enesco. And from her own studio came Copland, Thomson, Walter Piston, Roy Harris, and Marc Blitzstein. The artists who enriched her life and were enriched by it were the same artists who frequently caused the most excitement or brought the most pleasure to Carnegie Hall. The ovation she received was both for her and for those she represented in the Hall.

New music sets forth a new risk each time it is performed. There were many among the May, 1891, audience who thought Tchaikovsky's *Ouverture Solennelle 1812* was too daring for their taste. And when, in 1962, his newly reconstructed *Seventh Symphony* was performed in Carnegie Hall by Ormandy and the Philadelphia, it was also shrugged off by many listeners. Seventy-one years seemed but a moment in time; the more there was change, the more things remained the same. For those who love the old Hall, there is a lesson to be drawn: the past—so brilliant, so apparently matchless —was but a moment's prologue to what could be an even more exciting seventy years to come for the orchestras and men of Carnegie Hall.

3 * The Lady of Fifty-seventh Street

ON FORTY thousand square feet of land are piled four halls, approximately one hundred and seventy studios, thirty offices and apartments, and nine stores: the city within a city known as Carnegie Hall. One of New York's first all-fireproof buildings—iron, steel, brick and terracotta skeleton—Carnegie cost $763,531.25 to build and was assessed in 1891 at $500,000 (with the land). By 1925, when Robert E. Simon, Sr., bought it, the Hall was assessed at $1,850,000. During the Depression, when Simon was considering tearing it down for lack of rentals, it was worth $3,000,000 and bounded a sizable chunk of Simon real estate that ran east of Seventh Avenue, between Fifty-sixth and Fifty-seventh streets. Robert E. Simon, Jr., was stopped at the eleventh hour from converting the Hall into a parking lot and sold it to the City of New York for $5,000,000 in 1960.

But figures alone add little to a portrait of any building. Carnegie Hall is a remarkable memento of bygone architecture, a fascinating specimen of the eclectic school. Its mass is heavily German, its arches and facings are Greco-Roman, the treatment of the tiers and balconies reflects the baroque sweep of late Renaissance Italy; yet its skeleton typifies modern Franco-American engineering. Superficially Carnegie is a clumsy building. Predating ferroconcrete, its bearing walls run to four-and-a-half-foot thicknesses. A complete lavatory, for example, is *inside* a wall of the Recital Hall dressing room. This vast masonry and gener-

ous use of well seasoned wood could account for much of the Hall's resonance. Legend attributes the acoustics to a solid rock bed underneath. Actually, Carnegie is built over a bubbling spring-fed pond (once a watering spot for the foraging goats of Goat Hill); hydraulic pumps under the theater operate twenty-four hours a day to carry off the water.

This was a transition period in American architecture. Tuthill and Hunt, fashionably monumental, were also familiar with the airy interiors of the Frenchmen Eiffel and Boileau, who discovered the economy of cast-iron posts and steel beams. (James Bogardus was doing the same thing in New York, but recognition for him came late.) Using this inconspicuous form of support, Tuthill achieved the dramatic sweep and uninterrupted sight lines in the main hall. In the understage storage area the transitional feeling is most apparent. Here Tuthill employed Roman brick arches, later supported at intervals by cast-iron posts and steel beams. We can only guess at Hunt's contributions, but certain elements, such as the elevators and the decorative flora and fauna, are no doubt from his drawing board. Hunt earlier had designed New York's first artist studio-residence, with fourteen-foot windows and cathedral ceilings. These features also appear in the top floor of the original Carnegie building and in the upper floors of the rear (1894) and lateral (1896) buildings.

The mansard roof was squared off in 1894, with skylights added for still more studios, to

a. Lobby, looking east

b. Cocktail Lounge, formerly the Art Gallery

a. Chapter Hall

the delight of artists and photographers who have lived in them. Through the years these one-story and duplex studios have been altered. Additional plumbing and electrical lines were installed in the thirties, when residents were forced by the Depression to live where they worked. The four auditoriums, however, have remained virtually intact. Simon, Sr., had wanted to raise the parquet and fill the first floor with stores after the 1929 crash. He finally settled for a perimeter of nine stores. In 1948 the stage in Recital Hall, the best small hall in New York, was renovated and a large dressing room and reception area (the Rose Room, setting for Marion Rous's weekly "Philharmonic Forecasts") were connected to it on the floor below. Chapter Hall, capacity: 212, has changed not a whit. It is still a popular re-

b. Carnegie Lyceum

a. Storage area beneath the stage, Main Hall

hearsal hall, poetry center, synagogue, children's theater, and lodge hall.

In the basement of the lateral building, the sixteen-story tower on Fifty-seventh Street, were located a labyrinth of kitchens, a serving hall, icehouse, food-storage vaults, and several butler's pantries. Directly above this labyrinth was a large (capacity: 150) dining room. These facilities were rarely used; hence, in 1896, they were replaced by new steam boilers and electrical generators. The first floor dining room became an art gallery, used mainly by studio artist-tenants. At times a million dollars in art has hung there. In 1947 the Golub Brothers obtained a liquor license and turned the gallery into a cocktail lounge concession. Artists, however, have always shown there. Aside from a general sprucing up in 1960, this particular room has gone unchanged except that it is now called Café Carnegie.

The Carnegie Hall power plant was unique for its day. The steam frequently plagued vio-

b. The organ, the deck on which it rests, and the winch used to raise it through the stage floor

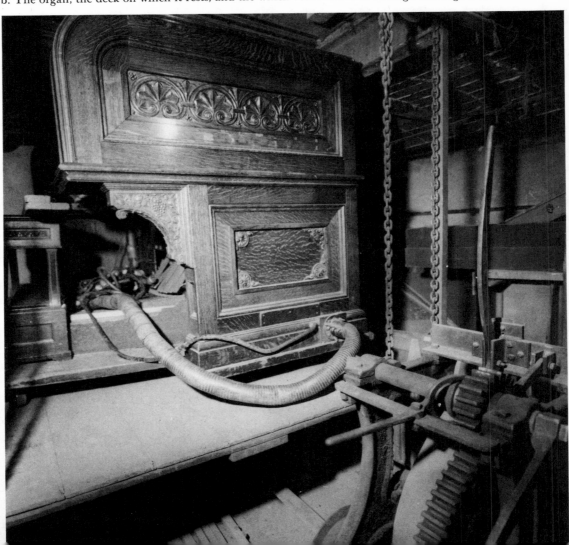

(above) Promenade behind first tier;
(below) Lounge behind second tier

linists; but the Hall, generating its own electricity, has never had a blackout. In addition, Carnegie boasted one of the first—and quite probably the longest-lasting—system of air cooling in a multistory building. A gigantic bunker in the basement was filled with ice and four large fans blew air across the bunker and on up through a network of masonry shafts and channels serving the four halls. On very hot nights, as much as 30 tons of ice per hour evaporated up through the walls. (These shafts served another purpose, too: when the Philharmonic roared through the Shostakovich *Fifth Symphony*, every student tenant could lean back and enjoy it.) In 1951 the first step toward a new system was made when the stage was air conditioned in the modern manner. Ten years later, after the Hall was again renovated by the Carnegie Hall Corporation, a steam-operated, lithium bromide absorption system was installed. The $275,000 system pumps 82,000 cubic feet of cooled air a min-

a. Main Hall ground floor, backstage area

b. Hallway behind first tier boxes

c. Second tier boxes

51

ute into the halls, automatically going on when the indoor temperature hits 72°. The installation now ensures Carnegie Hall as one of the finest year-round auditoriums in New York City.

Despite its many renovations and alterations, Carnegie Hall stands for an America of wealth and dash, of new-found national pride. Though many of its neighbors—Hunt or Stanford White châteaux—have since been sacrificed to commerce, this Hall remains, splendidly monumental. It was a monument conceived by a generation which had no radio, television, or motion pictures. There were fewer than 13,000 telephones in all New York in 1891. Young ladies passed the day pedaling their Winton two-wheelers around Central Park. The more reckless strolled down Broadway in boater hats and "rainy-daisy" skirts, the hemlines a provocative six inches from the ground. Money and art were intimate companions ("Railroads are the Rembrandts of investment," Henry Clay Frick liked to say), and *fin-de-siècle* mansions were resplendent with thick carpets, Moorish inlays, potted palms, and stones of Venice. Among these—extravagant in concept —admirable in execution—rose this temple of art: Carnegie Hall.

MUSIC HALL,

"URANIA,"

Every Monday and Wednesday Evening, at 8:15.
AND SATURDAY MATINEE.

The Seven Ages of our World,

From CHAOS to MAN.

The most interesting, instructive and novel entertainment
in New York.

Magnificent stage scenes, showing the original War of the elements,
the Outburst of Volcanic Fires, the Wonderful Primeval Ocean, the
Strange and Beautiful Landscapes of Antediluvian Times, the Gigantic
Monsters that preceded the human race, and the marvelous geological
revolutions that ended in the appearance of Man.

Explanatory Discourse by Mr. Garrett P. Serviss.

Scenery by Messrs. W. KRANZ, H. HARDER and O. WINKL
Mechanical Effects by Messrs. W. KRANZ and T. ROUGH.
Light Effects by Mr. J. C. MAYRHO

Scene I.—*Chaos.*
Scene II.—*The First Land.*
Scene III.—*The Devonian Age.—Volcanic Eruptio*
Scene IV.—*The Carboniferous Age.*
. . .—Illustrations of the Earliest Life Fo
and the Development of Continents
. . . of Coal.

8, DECEMBER
At 8.30 o'clock

Buffalo Jones
(COL. CHAS. J. JONES)

A wonderful account of the most remarkable
hunting expedition the world
has ever known

Illustrated with exceptionally clear Motion
Pictures

SUBJECT

Lassoing Wild Animals in Africa

TICKETS, $1.50

Mail orders .
Metropoli:
New Y.

MUSIC HALL.

GRAND CONCERT

FOR THE BENEFIT OF THE

Starving People of Russia

Saturday Evening, March 12, at 8:15.

The Symphony Orchestra of New York

WALTER DAMROSCH, Conductor
with the following renowned artists, who have
volunteered their services:

Mesdames EAMES and SCALCHI and Messrs. DE RES
and LASSALLE (*By kind permission Messrs. Abbey & Grau*.

Mr. ADOLPH BRODSKY,
(*Concert Master and Solo Violinist of the Symphony Orchestra of N*)

Mr. LEOPOLD GODOWSKY, Pianist, and others

PROGRAMME.—Part I.

Solennelle,—Symphony Orchestra.
Concert, No. II, F minor,   Mr. Leopold Godowsky.
     Mr. Adolph Brodsky.
uan,—Mr. Edouard De Reszke
for Strings in C,
Part II.   mphony Orchestra.

Messrs. Lassalle and Dé Re
Eames.

Tsch

THE FAMOUS
Countess
Schimmelmann

SPEAKS AND SING AT

CARNEGIE MUSIC HALL

Sunday Afternoon, December 10, 1899, at 2:30 sharp

—UNDER THE AUSPICES OF THE—

NEW YORK ANTI-SALOON LEAGUE

State and City Headquarters, 156 Fifth Avenue

JOHN LEWIS CLARK, Manhattan, Dist. Supt.

PROGRAMME
Conducted by Mr. Ha.

DR. CARL E. DUFFT
WILL SING AT

CARNEGIE HALL

Great Anti-Saloon Demonstration!

Motto for 1899.—"Let us emphasize points on which we agree, and a
subjects as to which we differ."

REV. J. Q. A. HENRY, State Superintendent
REV. JOHN LEWIS CLARK,

I. SONG SERVICE "New York Christian Home for
PRAYER   Dr. J. WILBUR CHAPMAN, D.D., Presiding.
Superintendent   MR. VICTOR H. BENKE, Organist
OPENING ADDRESS, "The Recessional,"
RITONE SOLO—   MR. RICHA
DR. CARL E. DUFF   "Onward, Christian Soldi
Her Grace
Country, 'Tis

States Min
He estimat
Human B

ch, have been
ser has contribut

the box office.
ue, between 10:30

Recollectio
. . . People"

PULAR p

sale .

4 * Prophets, Presidents and Protesters

Delphi on Fifty-seventh Street—a deep, upholstered cave where all the gods, sacred and profane, have been freely worshiped; an old brown pile, a pigeon's roost, a monticule of art in midtown, an odd marketplace for the bartering of truth and error; yet, Carnegie Hall has been the closest thing to Delphi that America has had for nearly four generations.

Mr. Carnegie believed in free discussion, free inquiry, and free fellowship. It was a cheery view of the social order, arrived at after years of struggle and craft and—most important —of friendship with the great men of his day. He was president of both the Philharmonic Symphony Society and the Oratorio Society. He was a patron of the Authors Club, among whose members were Brander Matthews, William Dean Howells, Henry Holt, Louis Marie Viaud ("Pierre Loti"), Edwin Arlington Robinson, and Albert Payson Terhune. The Club met on the ninth floor of the new Music Hall. The Barnard Club and the Chess Club also met in the Hall, as well as Masons and Rotarians, Knights of Columbus and of Pythias, Gold Star Mothers, Daughters of the American Revolution, Sons of Italy, and a number of British cousins. Before artists became squatters in the upper floors the rooms were rented for meetings, lectures, and hearty male fellowship. Serious events occurred in the Hall, too, made possible by the management's adherence to a laudable interpretation of the First Amendment: "If you got the money, you got the Hall." No questions asked.

Among the earliest men of distinction to appear on Carnegie's stage were Booker T. Washington and Mark Twain. Washington was there on March 3, 1896, to raise money for Tuskegee Institute and to recount his plan for increased industrial training for Negroes, a latter-day emancipation of twelve million Americans. George Foster Peabody remembered Washington's speeches as "finely responsive to his audience which was fully responsive to him." A direct, conversational speaker, Washington was applauded by the parquet, while shouts of "That's right, Booker" and "You've got him there, Mr. Washington" rang from the balconies. Washington spoke again at Carnegie on April 6, 1906, at a Lincoln memorial. Also onstage was Mark Twain, who, twelve days later at a benefit for the Robert Fulton Memorial Association, bowed out of "the lecturing business."

Presiding at the Fulton meeting was General Frederick Dent Grant, Ulysses' oldest son and friend of Twain. Albert Bigelow Paine, Twain's Boswell, relates that Carnegie Hall was "hung with bunting, the stage was banked and festooned with decorations of every sort. General Grant, surrounded by his splendidly uniformed staff, sat in the foreground, and behind was ranged a levee of foremost citizens of the republic. The [Old Guard] band played 'America' as Mark Twain entered, and the great audience rose and roared out its welcome.... The house was packed, and the applause was so recurrent and continuous that often his voice was lost in remote corners. It did not matter. The tales were familiar to hearers; merely to see Mark Twain, in his old age and in that splendid setting, relating them, was enough. The audience realized that it was witnessing the close of a heroic chapter in a unique career. . . ."

One other chapter of some importance was written in 1901. At this time Americans came to hear a twenty-six-year-old veteran of the Boer War who had just won a seat in Parliament in the "Khaki" election. The young man was the dashing Winston Leonard Spencer Churchill, newspaperman, graduate of Sandhurst and Harrow, and articulate in matters of bravery recollected in tranquillity.

Churchill arrived at a time when Americans —no longer amazed by the wonders of their own frontier—were looking toward Asia, Africa, and the Middle East for the stuff of an evening's titillation. One of the first and most popular bearers of romantic tidings was Dwight Elmendorf, a moustachioed traveler wise in the knowledge of fright, fancy, and photography. Mr. Elmendorf hurried between the Brooklyn Academy of Music and the snug Carnegie Lyceum, his portmanteau bulging with slides and notes of far-off wonders. In 1904 another landloper—goateed, debonair— took to the stage of the Lyceum armed with anecdotes, slides, and assorted marginalia. Burton Holmes soon drew a following of such proportions that he had to move upstairs into the larger main hall, where he presented his fascinating travelogues for the next half-century. Under the management of Walter Everest the "Burton Holmes Travelogues" continue, with Robert Mallet, André de la Varre, and others narrating the colorful film programs. Despite living-room television, such downtown programs never lose their appeal and are always well attended. One of the most fascinat-

Booker T. Washington speaking at Lincoln memorial meeting; Mark Twain is seated, hands down, in first row of speakers

ing in recent years was the February, 1960, "Film Record of Poland," produced by Julien Bryan, the dean of motion-picture travelogues. Bryan spliced together films of Poland taken between 1936 and 1959, including some footage of the Nazi occupation. But the most moving aspect was Bryan's personal detective work, revealed on the Carnegie screen. In 1959 he had returned to Poland and searched out those Poles who had appeared before his cameras as children a good twenty years before. For the February program, Bryan, through the magic of film editing, presented a visual record of modern history's toll on individual human beings.

Sixty years ago, horizons evaporated with alarming speed. Lieutenant Robert Edwin Peary sledged down from Greenland bearing meteorites and sketches of Eskimos and told his story to Carnegie crowds in 1897. (An Amer-

CARNEGIE HALL
THURSDAY EVENING, JANUARY 31, 1901
AT 8:30 O'CLOCK

LECTURE
—BY—
Mr. Winston Churchill, M.P.

SUBJECT
"The War As I Saw It"
Illustrated by Lantern Slides from Photos.

SYNOPSIS OF LECTURE

The Boer Military System—The Commando—The Party of Friends—Long Preparations—Vast Stores of Military Material—Formidable Nature of the British Task—Some Dangers which were avoided—The Situation in Natal last November—The Approaching Peril—Action of the Natal Ministry—"Worthy of Classic Times"—Estcourt—The Armoured Train—Once too often—Joubert's Advance—Fate of the Armoured Train—Prisoners of War—Behind Bulwana Hill—Pretoria.

My Escape—The Sentries and the Wall—Through

Programme continued on second page following

b. Winston Churchill in electric cab during first trip here

ican flag—and the standard of Delta Kappa Epsilon—he had left implanted in the polar snows.) Sixteen years later, Dr. Frederick Albert Cook was in the hall explaining that *he* had discovered the North Pole before Peary. In 1913 Roald Amundsen came to Carnegie with the story—verified—of how he beat Robert Scott to the South Pole. Sir Ernest Shackleton followed with details of *his* visit to the bottom of the earth. And as early as 1897 lectures on the evolution of this fascinating planet were given by Garret P. Serviss, who delighted New Yorkers with his wealth of pre-Einstein error.

In 1890 Henry Cabot Lodge announced, "From the Rio Grande to the Arctic Ocean there should be one flag and one country!"

This happy idea was accompanied by the rattle of American sabers south of the Rio Grande (Venezuela, Nicaragua, Panama) and west of the Rio Grande (the annexation of Hawaii and Samoa, and the Open Door to China) and east of the Rio Grande (the War with Spain). Moving through these restive, imperialistic years was Theodore Roosevelt.

The century's first new President, the "Sage of Sagamore" was a hearty, vigorous man whose squinting eyes seemed to see just a bit farther than anyone else's. Like his fellow Americans, he was insatiably curious about the world, eager to tear out its secrets with his own bold hands, yet bent on guarding it with his country's special brand of righteous

a. Robert E. Peary

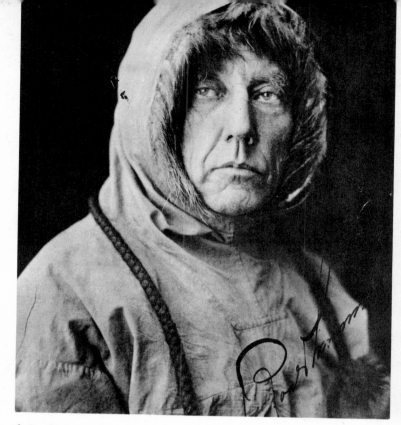

d. Roald Amundsen

b. Dr. Frederick Cook

c. Sir Ernest H. Shackleton

f. Richard E. Byrd

e. Amelia Earhart

59

Theodore Roosevelt

defense. Roosevelt was in and out of Carnegie Hall during most of his public life. He personally welcomed Admiral Dewey there in 1899. But in the 1912 election imbroglio, T.R. gave what many believe to have been his finest speech.

The Republicans were torn apart in 1912. "Fighting Bob" La Follette, architect of the Wisconsin Idea, was tirelessly—but ineffectively—rallying insurgent Republicans to his Progressive party. On January 22nd, Amos Pinchot rented Carnegie Hall for a La Follette speech. His brother Gifford chaired the meeting, which "was a very good meeting indeed, with several thousand people turned away." But the country was really waiting for Roosevelt to commit himself. Would he oppose Taft? Would he help the ailing La Follette off the murderous campaign trail? La Follette finally collapsed. A month later, T.R. shouted in Cleveland, "My hat's in the ring! The fight is on and I'm stripped to the buff!" A fellow Bull Mooser, Henry Luther Stoddard, however, recalls "another speech by Roosevelt . . . that brought him new popularity; it gave the key to the spirit that prompted him to get into the campaign. It was made at Carnegie Hall, March 20, to an audience that crowded that famous hall to the roof. . . . [Roosevelt] said: 'The leader for the time being, whoever he may be, is but an instrument to be used until broken and then cast aside; and if he is worth his salt he cares no more when he is broken than a soldier cares when he is sent where his life is forfeit in order that the victory may be won. In the long fight for righteousness, the watchword for all of us is, Spend and Be Spent. It is a little matter whether any one man succeeds or fails; but the cause shall not fail, for it is the cause of mankind. We here in America hold in our hands the hope of the world, the fate of the coming years; and the shame and disgrace will be ours if in our eyes the light of high resolves is dimmed, if we trail in the dust the golden hopes of man.' "

On November 5, 1912, T.R. polled 4,119,538 votes, topping Taft (Republican), Debs (Socialist), Chaffin (Prohibition), and Reimer (Socialist Labor). But the winner—with over six million votes—was Woodrow Wilson (Democrat).

Wilson's "New Freedom" was predicated on world peace. Peace was a subject also close to Andrew Carnegie's heart: he built the Peace Palace at The Hague, and established the Carnegie Endowment for International Peace. In the spring of 1907 Carnegie leased his own Hall for a week-long peace festival, assembling

Woodrow Wilson

a. Carnegie Peace Conference, 1907

b. Count Felix von Luckner

c. Floyd Gibbons

62

a. Mrs. Carrie Chapman Catt (standing center) addressing National American Woman Suffrage rally

on the platform everyone from Jane Addams to Rabbi Stephen Wise, President Theodore Roosevelt to William Jennings Bryan, Samuel Gompers to Princeton's President Woodrow Wilson. It was a grand, bold gesture. But it had no effect on history. In 1917, America's President Wilson reluctantly picked up the "Big Stick."

If any ghosts of the 1907 peace festival remained in Carnegie Hall, they were forthwith exorcized by hair-raising accounts of "Over There" given by Colonel Palmer and Sergeant York, Billy Bishop and Floyd Gibbons, Lowell Thomas, General O'Ryan, Pat O'Brien, and several regiments more. Wilson's only appearance in Carnegie while President took place the afternoon of July 9, 1919. He had debarked at Hoboken, then was ferried to Manhattan to report to the American people in Carnegie on the august decisions of Versailles.

It would seem that Carnegie Hall was a man's province, but that's not true at all. As far back as 1853, when Miss Lucy Stone showed her bloomers to the Women's Rights Convention, the ladies were on the warpath for equal rights. Historians accept 1910 as the year of the big *Putsch*, led by Carrie Chapman Catt, Anna Howard Shaw, and others. On January 12, 1912, Emmeline Pankhurst, the Bakunin

b. Mrs. Emmeline Pankhurst (with bouquet) and cadre

a. Edwin Markham　　　　　　　b. Rabindranath Tagore　　　　　　　c. William Butler Yeats

of the suffrage movement, staged a tumultuous Carnegie meeting. Mrs. O. H. P. Belmont and the gorgeous Inez Mulholland were inspired enough to lead a parade of liberated Sabines the length of Fifth Avenue a few months later. Harriet Stanton Blatch maintained the drum-fire with a mass meeting of the Women's Political Union in Carnegie, June 29, 1914. Then, in 1916, just before she was arrested for running a birth control clinic in Brooklyn, Margaret Sanger told a Carnegie audience her conception of family planning (*caveat actor*).

And there were moments of equal greatness when the dust was not thick in the air. These moments belonged to poets, artists, and novelists who have appeared in the Hall. Among the first were novelists John Watson (Ian Maclaren) and Alexander Black, who introduced into our lexicon the phrase "Miss America." In 1904 William Butler Yeats arrived on his first United States tour. *The Wanderings of Oisin* and his edition of Blake's verse were already known here. But he did not speak of Irish mythological characters (Countess Cathleen, Cuchulain, King Goll, or Queen Maeve); his subjects were the real Irish firebrands—Griffith and Parnell and the valiant band of Sinn Fein. Since then Carnegie has been host to Sir Rabindranath Tagore, Ilya Tolstoi, Maurice Maeterlinck, Hilaire Belloc, John Masefield, Langston Hughes, Ogden Nash and many more. Recital Hall, Chapter Hall, and

the Lyceum have been more popular for intimate readings, while the main hall frequently had a writer or two dress up a political or social gathering: Rex Stout on the first anniversary of Pearl Harbor, Louis Bromfield in a War Bond rally.

The teens and twenties were the peak years for public speaking. Topics were limitless and the audience was reasonably literate and decidedly inquisitive. A recent tide of immigration had also enriched the country with many Old-World intellectuals. New ideas were suddenly important, and those who advanced them were in great demand. The roll call of Carnegie orators includes such names as Albert Einstein, Bertrand Russell, Eugene Debs, Herbert Hoover, Scott Nearing, Will Rogers, and the two giants of liberal thought—Norman Thomas and Clarence Darrow.

Thomas was still a young divinity student when he first appeared on the Carnegie stage in 1908. He came dressed as "Father Knickerbocker," a character in a benefit for Christ Church. Later he took part in antiwar meetings, Socialist party rallies, as a candidate for governor and mayor, and in a score of lively debates. In 1944, Thomas, Herbert Hoover, and Connecticut's Lieutenant Governor Odell Shepard joined in a nonpartisan spare-the-children campaign inspired by Hoover.

Thomas recalls a 1921 meeting he moderated, featuring Morris Hillquit, cofounder with

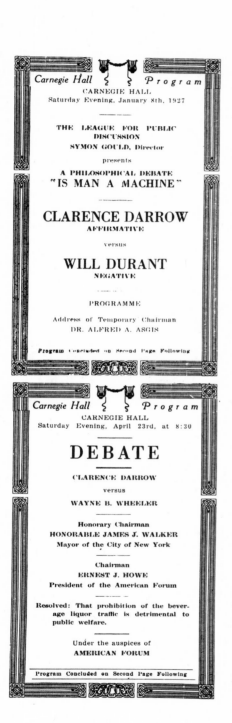

Carnegie Hall 〜 *Program*

CARNEGIE HALL
Saturday Evening, January 8th, 1927

THE LEAGUE FOR PUBLIC
DISCUSSION
SYMON GOULD, Director

presents

A PHILOSOPHICAL DEBATE
"IS MAN A MACHINE"

CLARENCE DARROW
AFFIRMATIVE

versus

WILL DURANT
NEGATIVE

PROGRAMME

Address of Temporary Chairman
DR. ALFRED A. ASGIS

Program Concluded on Second Page Following

Carnegie Hall 〜 *Program*

CARNEGIE HALL
Saturday Evening, April 23rd, at 8:30

DEBATE

CLARENCE DARROW

versus

WAYNE B. WHEELER

Honorary Chairman
HONORABLE JAMES J. WALKER
Mayor of the City of New York

Chairman
ERNEST J. HOWE
President of the American Forum

Resolved: That prohibition of the bever-
age liquor traffic is detrimental to
public welfare.

Under the auspices of
AMERICAN FORUM

Program Concluded on Second Page Following

Clarence Darrow

Debs and Victor Berger of the Social Democratic party (pro) and Clarence Darrow (con). They were to debate Charles Evans Hughes's protocol for United States participation in the World Court. The meeting was scheduled for 8:30. Hillquit and Thomas were on time; Darrow was not. There was stomping and clapping just before 9:00, when Darrow, in his customarily rumpled suit, burst upon the stage. Amid the applause, Darrow stepped up to Thomas and whispered, "Do you have a copy of the Hughes protocol?" Thomas asked, "Mr. Darrow, have you by any chance *not read* the Hughes protocol?" Apparently Darrow hadn't. But in a proud voice, easily heard by the first eight rows, Darrow replied, "Mr. Thomas, trust me. I can debate any question in the negative!" And he was right; the meeting was a roaring success. (*Footnote*: The United States did not joint the Court.)

Cynics and sophisticates have appeared regularly at the Hall, slapping society's wrist from this fine vantage point. But a simpler, rosier breed of orator has had his evening, also. The first optimist in Carnegie Hall was Elbert Hubbard, the seer of East Aurora, New York. He preached "good times ahead" from 1901 to 1915. His sunny career was cut short when he went down with the *Lusitania*. More optimists followed, however, including French psychotherapist Dr. Emile Coué. His auto-therapeutic slogan was: "Day by day, in every way, I am getting better and better." Not all Americans bought this idea, though; crowds of them returned to the Hall to witness meetings which possibly reflected the twentieth century with a greater accuracy: antisaloon meetings, anti-Kaiser, anti-Franco, and anti-Nazi rallies, anti-Communist and anti-McCarthy protest rallies, and scores of revolution anniversaries. It was common for leaflets to be tossed over the balcony rail and float to the parquet, where the center aisle was no-man's-land between warring camps. Arguments raged behind the first and second tiers and rumors of pickets scuffling on Fifty-seventh Street made the old Hall a haven indeed for those who were safe inside. Picasso on the telephone brought the crowd to its feet. Raymond Massey inspired bravos for Czech Independence Day. Lithuanian emigrés wept for their homeland and cheered Grand Duke Vytantas. Mayor La Guardia joined Frank Sinatra for a One World Award. Alexandr Fadeev praised his Soviet Writers Union—then went back to Moscow and commited suicide.

For decades the Hall has held firm despite the great tempests that roared within. Yet, through it all has run a certain democratic sanity; the First Amendment was fiercely exer-

---

a. Evangelist meeting, 1900's; "tents" reflect New York's melting-pot population

b. Evangeline and William Bramwell Booth

a. Dwight Moody

b. "Gypsy Smith"

cised here; this free, uncensored stage was its greatest monument.

Actually the Hall was opened in 1891 not to the sound of inflamed oratory but to the soothing prayers of Episcopal Bishop Henry Codman Potter. Potter was an eminent churchman, the prime mover behind the building of another great New York structure, the Cathedral of St. John the Divine. From Potter down to the present day, Carnegie has been a house of worship or celebration for every sect.

In 1898 Roman Catholics sat in Carnegie Hall watching a pioneering motion picture of a day in the life of Pope Leo XIII. (An annual event has been the showing of slides at Eastertime of great paintings of the life of Christ, admission free.) In 1900 one of the largest of all religious meetings was held: a memorial to Dwight Lyman Moody, the evangelist-educator who had died the year before. Moody's helpmate, Ira David Sankey, organist, singer, and prolific composer of hymns, led the overflow meeting in eulogies. Annie Wood Besant, the British theosophist, came to the Hall in 1909 from her adopted India. Most recently, Dr. Irvin Seale conducted Sunday morning Church of the Truth services in the main hall and held study sessions in a studio suite on the ninth floor. Currently, the principal religious tenant is the Church of Divine Unity, led by the Reverend Helen Zagat.

The Booths, founders of the Salvation Army, came here from England to address mass fund-raising rallies in the Hall; New York's leading citizens attended. But then the British were always successful at this. Sir Oliver Lodge and Sir Arthur Conan Doyle came over right after World War I to conduct mass spirtualist meetings. Oddly enough, Carnegie Hall has been especially hospitable to spiritualists and kindred sects. Swami Yogananda was quite popular during the thirties, with programs devoted to "Harnessing Cosmic Consciousness for Unfailing Success." Up in Studio 1010 the Truth Forum, founded by "Brother John," has had a lively history. In the midst of the furor about the preservation of the Hall, the Forum's leader, the Reverend Jennie Moore, calmly invited one and all to hear the Reverend Fred Ide of Bath, New York, explain his "unique

a. Bishop Henry Potter

b. Annie Besant

c. Dr. Irvin Seale

d. Dr. Harry Emerson Fosdick

mediumship." "During the healing period of the Truth Forum," the Reverend Moore promised, "Reverend Ide will also demonstrate his rose healing technique. Bring a rose to the meeting. We promise you a most enlightening —even a surprising—evening in spirit revelation." (The following week, the Reverend Moore explained "metamotion.")

Among the Jews of New York, Carnegie Hall is also a well loved meeting place. Cantor Josef Rosenblatt appeared there first in 1918 and frequently thereafter. In 1924 the leading cantors of the northeast gathered on stage to honor the famed Don Fuchs, Chief Cantor of Vienna. Sidor Belarsky and Mascha Benya have held traditional Hanukkah celebrations in the main hall. The twenty-fifth anniversary of the Yiddish radio commentator Mitchell Levitsky was observed here, also, with Cantors Hershkovitz, Koussevitzky, Aroni, and Schiendele joined by such non-Jewish friends as Nick Kenny. And in 1960, Cleveland's Rabbi Abba Hillel Silver (whose influence at the United Nations helped bring about the partitioning of Palestine into Israel and Jordan) led the celebration of the Theodor Herzl Centennial in the great Carnegie auditorium.

Rabbi Stephen S. Wise

For American Jewry, the establishment of the Free Synagogue by Dr. Stephen Samuel Wise (then thirty-six years old) was a major event. Four years later, in 1910, Dr. Wise moved the Free Synagogue to Carnegie Hall. From that august pulpit Rabbi Wise conducted services and delivered powerful sermons in the cause of Reformed Judaism and Zionism.

The Free Synagogue has since moved crosstown, but Rabbi Stephen Rosenblatt (no re-lation to the cantor) has for a dozen years used Chapter Hall as his Temple B'nai Sholom (Temple of the Children of Peace). Here he has conducted weekly services—and occasional weddings—for the shopkeepers and artists in the Carnegie vicinity.

When Rabbi Stephen Wise died in 1949, he lay in state in the main hall. The event drew such large crowds that Fifty-seventh Street was closed to traffic. But actually, he was not the first to be so honored. Sidney Hillman, cofounder of the CIO and frequent Carnegie orator, was whisked to the Hall just hours after his death in the summer of 1946. Arrangements had been made hastily over the phone with House Manager John Totten, who then sped from his Long Island retreat to take charge. However, when he arrived, the Hall was already packed with thousands of labor's rank and file, come to view the still shell of a former New Deal champion.

The Wise and Hillman funerals were impressive affairs. They rated good newspaper coverage. But another event—possibly more moving than any of its type—caused barely a ripple in the press. It was the September, 1961, memorial meeting for Arthur Zygelboim. An urn containing his ashes rested on the stage (after the meeting the ashes were interred in a corner of a Brooklyn cemetery). Zygelboim was a Polish Jew who escaped to London during the war and unsuccessfully tried to get the Allies to help the Jews still left in Eastern

a. Rabbi Stephen Rosenblatt in Chapter Hall

b. *Sholom* after the service

Bruno Walter conducts the Max Reinhardt memorial, powerful anti-Nazi program of 1944

Europe. In despair Zygelboim committed suicide, hoping his martyrdom would arouse Britons and Americans to action. It didn't. In 1961, the Workmen's Circle and the Jewish Labor Bund, witnessing angry outbursts of anti-Semitism in America, West Germany, and the Soviet Union, brought the ashes of Zygelboim to New York and invoked his memory in a new hour of trial. A guard of honor lined the stage: escapees of the Warsaw ghetto, other Jewish partisans, and a scattering of concentration camp survivors. But this did not impress the world; the passionate speeches, the hurtful memories hardly penetrated Carnegie's thick walls. Had the mass meeting gone out of style?

Certainly the crowd-pleasers have gone—the Darrows, the Hillmans, and the Coués. Gone are such Carnegie orators as Senator Albert J. ("March of the Flag") Beveridge; Emma Goldman, the fiery anarchist; Mayor La Guardia; the nasal Kansas Communist, Earl Browder; Senator William E. ("The Great Opposer") Borah; and a host of others who liked to talk directly to people they could reach out and touch. As a forum, Carnegie Hall—like most halls today—has fallen on dull days; radio and television is a much safer and sometimes even cheaper way to run a "mass meeting." In the Hall today the annual meeting of automotive engineers drones on where Ralph Bellamy narrated the Freedom Diary. The Salesperson of the Year and the Best Annual Report awards are presented to Junior Achievement where Dr. Harry Emerson Fosdick launched the Good Will Congress.

The passions of the mass meeting may well have been interred with the ashes of Arthur Zygelboim.

Labor leaders bid Hillman a last farewell

a. William Shores arriving at the Hall

b. Preparing backstage

c. Arpad Sandor at the piano, Dale McKechnie turning pages

d. Final bow for an appreciative audience

e. Greeting friends in Rose Room

f. The début is history

5 * Solo Genius

A CARNEGIE debut usually consists of a young artist, his manager, a few friends, and lots of courage, all marshaled together in Recital Hall—modest, intimate, and cheap. On a crisp Sunday afternoon in March, 1960, the young baritone William Shores, graduate of the Juilliard School of Music (Master of Science in Voice) had his official coming-out in this pleasant auditorium. His program was—because it *had* to be—varied and difficult: songs by Gluck, Brahms, Vásquez, Fauré, Virgil Thomson and others sung in French, German, Spanish and English, plus a group of traditional American spirituals. Arpad Sandor, a seasoned accompanist and himself a popular recitalist, was on hand at the piano; fellow music student and friend Dale McKechnie helpfully turned pages. Concert Manager Norman Seaman took care of all details, gambling on getting back his costs plus 50 percent of any profit. (This kind of liberal financial arrangement is *a*typical.) At the last moment, all hands tried "papering the hall"; that is, they gave away tickets to friends and relatives to fill the few remaining seats—a time-honored custom. Aided by a thermos of tea, calmly sipped during intermission, Mr. Shores bore up through his two hours, then went down to the Rose Room to receive well-wishers. Five hours later the *Times* said (in 2½ inches): "He sang in a straightforward manner displaying a voice that had a pleasant, deep quality, marred by a considerable amount of wobble. His approach to the music was serious, sometimes effective, often stiff." The *Tribune* (in

3½ inches) said: "Although the voice *per se* is neither especially large, nor wide-ranging, nor colorful, Mr. Shores' style-awareness and intelligence go far as compensating factors." Both reviews—one initialed, the other unsigned—were by young critics making their debuts, too, in their own field. (*Footnote:* Mr. Shores is still singing and has added piano performances to his programs.)

Although Carnegie Hall was officially opened on May 5, 1891, it was virtually in mothballs during its first summer. The box seats went to Newport; the balcony went to Coney. The first season really began on November 13th with Beethoven's *Seventh* and Brahms's *Violin Concerto*, concertmaster Adolf Brodsky as soloist. But this is far less important than the event on the 17th, the appearance of the first recitalist in Carnegie Hall: Ignace Jan Paderewski. The young Polish virtuoso had triumphed at the Paris Exposition of 1889, and a year later won from Londoners, especially the ladies, unbridled admiration. The Steinway Company, which had closed its Fourteenth Street hall in 1890, brought Paderewski to America as it had brought Anton Rubinstein twenty years before. (In Europe, however, Paderewski played an Erard.) It was a bold stroke and a profitable one: Paderewski brought in a million dollars on this 22,000-mile *tournée* of the United States. He appeared 117 times in public and a dozen times in private "Bohemian" parties staged by the Vanderbilt-Astor set. With his shock of golden-red hair and his romantic and courteous manner, Paderewski reduced his New York début audience to ecstasy. They mobbed him on stage, snipped his hair, kissed his hands and clothing, and exalted him with very un-Victorian fervor. Oddly enough, the Steinway Company had felt unsure and had "papered" the hall for the 17th. But for the following night's recital, all free invitations were called in, twice as many chairs were crammed into the boxes, and Carnegie Hall had its first smash sellout. It was also Paderewski's thirty-first birthday.

After touring the country in a private railroad car, complete with personal grand piano, Paderewski returned to Poland. During World War I he abandoned the piano to work for war relief and Polish independence. From the Versailles meeting with Wilson came the thirteenth (Polish freedom) of the famous Fourteen Points.

Paderewski returned to this country briefly as ambassador in 1918 and became Poland's first premier in 1919. Three years later, on November 22, 1922, Paderewski was back at Carnegie Hall to begin a triumphant recital tour of the United States. World War II once again tore him from his music. He was President of the Polish Government-in-Exile until his death in New York, June 29, 1941. Only five months before, the United States celebrated "Paderewski Week," the fiftieth anniversary of his career in America.

The Paderewski success of 1891 established

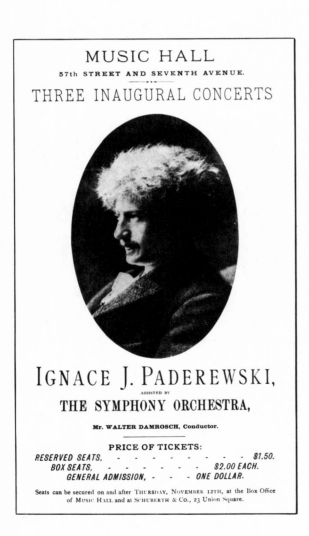

MUSIC HALL

57th STREET AND SEVENTH AVENUE.

THREE INAUGURAL CONCERTS

IGNACE J. PADEREWSKI,

ASSISTED BY

THE SYMPHONY ORCHESTRA,

Mr. WALTER DAMROSCH, Conductor.

PRICE OF TICKETS:

RESERVED SEATS, - - - - - - - $1.50.
BOX SEATS, - - - - - - $2.00 EACH.
GENERAL ADMISSION, - - - ONE DOLLAR.

Seats can be secured on and after THURSDAY, NOVEMBER 12TH, at the Box Office of MUSIC HALL and at SCHUBERTH & Co., 23 Union Square.

FIRST CONCERT,

TUESDAY EV'G, NOVEMBER 17TH, 1891,

AT 8.15 O'CLOCK.

PROGRAMME.

1. OVERTURE—*In Springtime,* . . . . GOLDMARK

   ORCHESTRA.

2. CONCERTO—No. 2, in G minor, ... CAMILLE SAINT-SAËNS

   Andante sostenuto. Allegro scherzando. Presto.

   IGNACE J. PADEREWSKI.

3. AIRS DE BALLET from *Iphigenie en Aulide,* . . . . GLUCK

   ORCHESTRA.

4. PIANO SOLI—*a,* Nocturne,
       b, Prelude,
       c, Valse, ... FRED. CHOPIN
       d, Etude,
       e, Ballade,

   IGNACE J. PADEREWSKI.

   INTERMISSION.

5. CONCERTO—No. 1, Op. 17, ... IGNACE J. PADEREWSKI

   Allegro. Romanza. Allegro molto vivace.

   IGNACE J. PADEREWSKI.

6. "RIDE OF THE VALKYRIES," . . . . WAGNER

   ORCHESTRA.

Steinway & Sons' Pianos used at these Concerts.

Carnegie Hall as a most desirable place for musicians to appear. Yet, some skepticism remained; many European artists had misgivings about appearing in a "Music Hall," as Carnegie Hall was then called. ("Music Hall Founded By Andrew Carnegie" still remains above the Fifty-seventh Street marquee.) Reports of spiritualists, adventurers, and actresses using the stage seemed to confirm the questionable status of the Hall. Some Europeans equated New York's "Music Hall" with London's Pavilion Music Hall, where in 1891 Albert Chevalier was belting out things like "The Coster's Serenade" and "My Dear Old Dutch." The management, aware of this drawback, began calling their property Carnegie Hall.

Among the earliest recitalists were Vladimir de Pachmann, Eugène Ysaÿe, Adolf Brodsky, Maud Powell, and composer-pianist Edward MacDowell. (From MacDowell's programs in Recital Hall came the nucleus of Columbia University's Department of Music.) Child prodigies abounded then as now. The Metropolitan, however, had the honor of introducing an eleven-year-old who was to become the leading pianist of the twenties: Josef Hofmann. An instant success, Hofmann followed his debut with almost fifty concerts. Then the Society for the Prevention of Cruelty to Children stepped in and charged Hofmann *père*, who was also Josef's teacher, with "exploitation." The Hofmanns sailed for Europe, where Josef studied under the ubiquitous Anton Rubinstein. In 1898 he returned to America for good and made Carnegie Hall his recital headquarters. He dazzled colleagues with his interpretations of Chopin, Schumann, and Beethoven. As teacher, friend, and exponent of American works, Hofmann encouraged and gave stature to the musical talent of his adopted country.

Although the Opera House first presented the young Hofmann, Carnegie can boast of introducing another eleven-year-old to New York: Yehudi Menuhin on November 25, 1927. His hands were too small to tune his three-quarter Grancino fiddle; the concertmaster smilingly obliged. Under the direction of Fritz Reiner, Menuhin plunged into the

Ignace Jan Paderewski

Souvenir à Me g.
Mrs Frank W. Sanger
de
Josef Hofmann
N.Y. 27/3 88.

a. Eugène Ysaÿe

b. Maud Powell

Beethoven *Violin Concerto*, brilliantly executed the difficult Joachim cadenza, and received a wild ovation. The boy was the equal of any man.

Carnegie *Wunderkinder* are legion: Erica Morini at fifteen, Michael Rabin at fourteen, Bela Szilágyi at thirteen, Lorin Hollander at eleven, Ruggiero Ricci at nine, Ferrucio Burco at eight, Joseph Alfidi at seven. Some prodigies in Europe were late in coming to the Hall: Wanda Landowska at forty-nine, Rudolf Serkin at thirty-three, Myra Hess at thirty-two. They are, however, the "tritons among the minnows," who, unlike many artists today, were

able to mold an audience to their art—not the reverse. There are other differences, too.

Until the early thirties the recitalist had nothing but his instrument between him and his audience: no microphones, control rooms, mixers, filters, or amplifiers. Yet, each instrument can, when properly employed, send its message for great distances. However, the most difficult one is carried by every human being: the "voice box." It is perhaps significant that the Oratorio Society was the first permanent tenant of Carnegie Hall, performing under the Damrosch brothers and Albert Stoessel. A

a. Dame Myra Hess

b. Mischa Elman

c. Jascha Heifetz

a. Yehudi Menuhin

b. Wanda Landowska

c. Rudolf Serkin

A performance of Handel's *Messiah*

sensitive, able musician, Stoessel took over the Society in 1921 at age twenty-seven and stayed with it until his death in 1943. The Society (as of 1963) had sung Handel's *Messiah* over a hundred and forty times—something of a record—earning the continued respect and love of New Yorkers throughout the years. The mention of Handel brings to mind the Cantata Singers, who gave the first complete performance in New York of the dramatic oratorio *Belshazzar* in 1960, Thomas Dunn conducting. Not all choruses need orchestral accompaniment, however. Certainly the Original Don Cossack Chorus, under the ageless Serge Jaroff, has been a much-admired Carnegie regular since its first program in 1930. (In its repertoire is "The History of the Don Cossack Chorus in Song: Revolution—Civil War—Flight—Detention Camp—Famine—Epidemic—Rise to the Present Time," an impressive musical diary.)

The list of the choruses which have appeared at Carnegie Hall is long and admirable: the Westminster Choir, Vienna Boys Choir, Down Town Glee Club, Harvard-Radcliffe Glee Clubs, and the excellent Dessoff Choirs. The Dessoff Choirs—160 to 170 voices strong—have been singing in Carnegie Hall for all their 36-year history; their brilliant Swiss conductor, Paul Boepple, founded the Cantata Singers in 1934, and then moved on to the Dessoff group three years later. To recall any one chorus may be unfair; yet, a group with excellent credentials and an exciting record of accomplishment almost exclusively in Carnegie Hall is the Schola Cantorum.

Although the name is over 1,500 years old, the Schola Cantorum of New York was first formed in 1909. Gustav Mahler was then resident musical director at Carnegie and he needed a women's chorus to assist in a performance of "Sirens," the third of Debussy's three *Nocturnes*. Kurt Schindler had just organized a forty-voice women's chorus from among the MacDowell Club membership and he offered their services to Mahler. The conductor was pleased with their performance and encouraged Schindler to make the chorus permanent. Schindler expanded it to two hundred mixed voices, including some professionals. In 1929 Hugh Ross became director and has since led the Schola through a con-

tinuous series of virtuoso performances. An
early peak evening was its 1938 performance
of Verdi's *Requiem* with the Philharmonic
under Toscanini. As Olin Downes reported in
the *Times* the next day, "Superlatives are not
only dangerous but wearisome. Yet, it must be
said that this was very nearly the perfect performance. . . . The effect was overwhelming."
As for the Schola itself: "Last night it established a new record for itself, as regarded clean
intonation, even in unaccompanied passages,
technical finish, and, above all, feeling." (Very
often, the reviews of the Schola Cantorum and
the Boston Symphony Orchestra have been
strikingly similar—which is still another measure of the group's excellence.) Ross and the
Schola have also been outstanding in their
desire and ability to perform modern compositions. The Schola has premiered such pieces
as Samuel Barber's *Prayers of Kierkegaard*,
Ernest Bloch's *Jewish Sabbath Service*, and
Heitor Villa-Lobos' symphonic poem *Manu-
Carara*.

Despite its spaciousness, the main hall does
lend an air of intimacy to the solo performance,
also. The décor may be rich, yet it was sculpted
to human scale. Above all, the excellent acoustics establish the ideal one-to-one ratio between
singer and each auditor. Among the early singers to appear in Carnegie and enjoy its com-
patibility were Metropolitan stars Clémentine
de Vere, Olive Fremstad, Heinrich Heyn, Emil
Fischer, and Italo Campanini. (Campanini
opened the Hall by singing in the May, 1891,
festival; he also sang in the first performance
—*Faust*—by the Metropolitan company in their
new Opera House, October, 1883.) In 1904
Canadian tenor Edward Patrick Johnson (he
dropped the Patrick later, and also the pseu-
donym Edoardo di Giovanni) made his début
at Carnegie. (In 1922 he joined the Metropolitan and in 1935 began a fifteen-year career
as its popular manager.)

In 1910 a young man more Irish than Johnson gave his first Carnegie recital to a sellout
house. John McCormack had arrived in this
country scarcely a year before as the protégé
of Oscar Hammerstein I, who was then fighting to keep open his Manhattan Opera House,
vigorous rival of the Metropolitan. McCormack

a. John McCormack

b. Russell Oberlin

c. Roland Hayes

d. Paul Robeson

83

excelled in Irish music, but was most widely known for his rendition of "At Dawning," the C. W. Cadman melody based on Indian themes. Another Carnegie recitalist, Alma Gluck, was also associated with a Cadman song, "From the Land of the Sky-Blue Water." Among the male voices to fill Carnegie Hall successfully, one of the most impressive—and controversial—has been that of Paul Robeson, a husky (All-American end), perceptive (Phi Beta Kappa) artist, who had his Carnegie début on November 5, 1929. This was in the middle of a calamitous two-week period. Seven days earlier—"Black Tuesday"—the canyons of Wall Street echoed with the crash of the stock market. Eight days later, November 13th, the bottom was reached. The Robeson program of art songs and spirituals seemed, under the circumstances, singularly frivolous.

Since then Robeson has had a stormy career, though the storms have been largely political. And when he returned to Carnegie on May 9, 1959 (after an eleven-year absence), a cordon of police stood by to avert trouble. None took place; politically, Robeson was becalmed. But once on stage, the sixty-year-old Robeson displayed an ageless vitality. In this May program Robeson gave the final speech of Othello, a role he starred in from 1943 to 1945:

Soft you; a word or two before you go.
I have done the state some service, and
they know't.
No more of that. I pray you, in your
letters,
When you these unlucky deeds relate,
Speak of me as I am; nothing extenuate,
Nor set down aught in malice. . . .

Enrico Caruso

Feodor Ivanovich Chaliapin

The brightest jewel in the crown of Heinrich Conried, then director of the Metropolitan, was Enrico Caruso. Caruso arrived in 1903 and made his début on November 23rd as the Duke in *Rigoletto*. He packed the Opera House twice a week (one night was always Monday, "Gala Night") ; then packed the 17,000-seat Hippodrome (shortly before McCormack did the same); and eventually packed Carnegie Hall. His May 23, 1918, appearance is still remembered with awe. It was a Red Cross benefit and also featured Jascha Heifetz and Sergei Rachmaninoff. It is difficult to conceive of a trio more handsomely endowed.

Caruso shares laurels with another singer who appeared often at Carnegie, a highly individual and controversial artist, basso Feodor Chaliapin. Chaliapin was born in Kazan, Russia, on February 11, 1873, exactly two weeks before Caruso was born in Naples, Italy. Conried, hearing reports of Chaliapin's success at La Scala, invited him to the Metropolitan. He first appeared November 20, 1907, in the title role of Boito's *Mefistofele* and ruffled his New York hosts. With the earthy realism of his friend Maxim Gorky, Chaliapin stepped on stage practically nude in the Bröcken scene. Critics like Henry Krehbiel of the *Tribune* frowned on Chaliapin's "vulgarity," his "disgusting frankness." He, in turn, was appalled at America's superficial understanding of opera. He left five months later.

Things went better in Europe. He conquered Berlin (his conductor, thirty-six-year-old Serge Koussevitzky), then London (his conductor, thirty-four-year-old Thomas Beecham), finally returned to America and the Metropolitan, then directed by Conreid's successor and his good friend of La Scala days, Giulio Gatti-Casazza. (Caruso had died four months before.) Chaliapin, under Sol Hurok's management, sang throughout the United States during the twenties and thirties, with Carnegie recitals included in each tour. He always drew capacity audiences, who marveled at the Russian giant (6'4", 225 lbs.). "Sometimes this remarkable man," said critic Olin Downes, "appears as an actor *manqué*. He acts with his voice as well as with his body; he seizes on the slightest excuse to envisage a moment that the observer always remembers. This is surely one of Mr. Chaliapin's greatest achievements—a remarkable example of action, gesture, facial expression and treatment of tone to give as much distinction as possible to the text. A virtuoso exhibition, one which achieved the status of great art."

Most of the great male voices in Carnegie Hall were primarily Opera House voices. But every now and then the public was surprised.

a. Lilli Lehmann

b. Emma Calvé

c. Mary Garden

Giovanni Buitoni, the head of the International Buitoni-Perugina Corporation (spaghetti, noodles, candy, etc.), had been dispensing awards at Carnegie Hall's annual Festival of San Remo, a gala of Italian songs and singers (both imported for the occasion). Then, on November 27, 1961, Signor Buitoni stepped upon the stage and unrolled his passionate basso voice in his concert debut. Gathered about him were such Italian stars as Licia Albanese (with whom he sang) and opera commentator Milton Cross.

The men, however, shared the stage with the ladies. From its very first season Carnegie has presented its audience with beauty—beauty of voice, of face and figure, of dress, and above all beauty of manner. These beloved women swept parquet, boxes, and balcony into a rich musical embrace. They shared with their listeners a world of romance, courage, and verve; a world in which Paris, Rome, Berlin, London and Vienna were, well before the air age, contiguous neighborhoods. New Yorkers rode their carriages between Carnegie and the Opera House to hear the greatest divas of the day: Emma Eames, Amelita Galli-Curci, Lillian

d. Mme. Luisa Tetrazzini

a. Lillian Nordica

b. Mme. Ernestine Schumann-Heink

c. Dame Nellie Melba

d. Lotte Lehmann

e. Marian Anderson

f. Renata Tebaldi

Sergei Rachmaninoff

Nordica (and her snippy poodle, "Turk"), Lucrezia Bori, Rosa Ponselle, Kirsten Flagstad, Birgit Nilsson, Leontyne Price, Joan Sutherland, and others. Thanks to the American Opera Society, Carnegie Hall's repertoire is almost as extensive as that of the Metropolitan and assuredly more daring. Carnegie does not have the backstage area or machinery to fly sets, but it has far better acoustics than does the Opera House, unimpeded sight lines (also better than the Opera House), and it offers the singer a chance to display a command of the art of song.

Despite the great performances of singers the catalogue of brilliance at Carnegie Hall is weighted heavily toward pianists. Over the past several decades, giants of music regularly gave their piano recitals in Carnegie. The Hall is, to a great extent, a testing place for professionalism. The true artist, once familiar with this auditorium, will play on its acoustics as carefully as he will on his instrument. (Says Dame Myra Hess: "I can play softer here than anywhere else.") Many recitalists, returning to the Hall year after year, attain a certain "recital proficiency" that is difficult to equal.

Leopold Godowsky was such a pianist. He was, it might be noted, among the first pianists heard here, on April 24, 1891, two weeks before the Hall officially opened. Godowsky was then twenty-one (his concert career actually began at age nine in Poland) and on the faculty of the New York College of Music. Until the tragic paralysis of his left hand, Godowsky gave some of the most talked-about recitals in the Hall.

Among Godowsky's close friends was a quiet, slim young Russian with the manner and musical feeling of a poet: Sergei Rachmaninoff. He was barely nineteen when he wrote his *Prelude in C-Sharp Minor,* twenty when he wrote his opera *Aleko,* and thirty-six when he came to the United States for a grand tour. At his November, 1909, Carnegie début he introduced his *Third Piano Concerto.* For the next thirty years he appeared on the stage in his three roles ("hunting three hares," as he sometimes called it) of composer-conductor-pianist. One of his most famous concerts was with Heifetz on a 1925 program honoring—

and featuring—the teacher of teachers, violinist Leopold Auer.

Benno Moiseiwitsch, a romanticist at the piano, gave a sellout recital in March, 1958; the box-office gross was $9,000. He performed three Rachmaninoff concertos with the Symphony of the Air under Leon Barzin. The audience called him back for six bows. Critics the next day poured out columns of superlatives. The *Post*'s Harriet Johnson was typical: "He played not only with an airborne fluency and accuracy, but with a poetry that transported the spirit momentarily far from the clang and distortions of a sky-rocketing world. . . . It was a jewel of a thousand colors perfectly cut."

Artists are inclined to be opinionated, but few are as verbally so as was Artur Schnabel. "Aristocratic" is the adjective usually associated with his programs. He sniffed at the "salon music" of Liszt and Chopin. His meat and drink were Beethoven, Schubert, Brahms, and Mozart. He demanded the very best from himself, from fellow artists, and from audiences, too. In 1935 he gave seven consecutive

Leopold Godowsky

a. Benno Moiseiwitsch

concerts of all thirty-two Beethoven sonatas, a memorable virtuoso performance. The Carnegie audience knew enough to bring the scores with them; Abram Chasins recalls that this was more important for entry than having a ticket!

One of the strangest débuts of all was that of young Vladimir Horowitz. In 1928 he fought Sir Thomas Beecham through the Tchaikovsky *B-Flat Minor*. "I played louder, faster, and more notes than Tchaikovsky wrote," he said later, "and there are plenty of notes in the concerto!"

Simon Barere—like Horowitz, a pupil of Felix Blumenfeld—was a comparative latecomer to the concert stage, but made up in flawless technique for what he lacked in concert personality. During his 1951 Carnegie appearance with Ormandy and the Philadelphia, in the midst of the Grieg *Piano Concerto*, Simon Barere suffered a heart attack and died onstage.

b. Artur Schnabel

a. Vladimir Horowitz

b. Simon Barrere

Artur Rubinstein

Artur Rubinstein is an original musician and a keen, many-sided personality. The 1921-1922 season was his first at Carnegie. After a period in Europe he returned in 1937 (under Sol Hurok's management) bearing Stravinsky's *Petrouchka Suite* (dedicated to Rubinstein). Its premiere was a triumph for both composer and performer. Rubinstein celebrated the twenty-fifth anniversary of his return by playing ten Carnegie concerts in forty days for the benefit of eleven charities. But he had done this sort of thing before: beginning on February 7, 1956, he gave five concerts in thirteen days, playing seventeen pieces for piano and orchestra by Grieg, Chopin, Mozart, Tchaikovsky, Rachmaninoff, Liszt, Schumann, Franck, and De Falla, *plus* all the concertos in the Brahms and Beethoven libraries.

Rubinstein's manager, Sol Hurok, describes the scene in the Carnegie Green Room after a Rubinstein concert: "The door is opened and the room suddenly shrinks in size as the people pour in, always too many. One after another he greets them, remembering the name, the face, even the language of each, darting about among his seven tongues and delightedly at home in each . . . his eloquent face and hands in constant motion. . . . Not all artists know the art of communicating with people. Rubinstein has made this art peculiarly his own."

Rubinstein excels in Chopin, but the distinction is not solely his. Alexander Brailowsky, a reserved scholar of the piano, early established his reputation by performing at Carnegie a six-concert cycle of Chopin's 169 pieces. Many consider Brailowsky to be the only true interpreter of Chopin since Paderewski. (Brailowsky and Paderewski were both students of Theodor Leschetizky.)

Robert Marcel Casadesus, who has brilliantly championed the music of impressionists Debussy and Ravel, is not only an articulate pianist-composer-teacher, but is the head of a rather remarkable family. His wife Gaby has frequently joined him in sparkling duo-piano performances. (One is inevitably reminded of the Lhevinnes, Josef and Rosina, who celebrated forty years of keyboard partnership at a Carnegie recital in January, 1939, and of

Rubinstein at rehearsal; photo taken through Main Hall stage ceiling

a. Alexander Brailowsky

Vitya Vronsky and Victor Babin, who celebrated their twenty-five years together in the Hall in February, 1962.) Most recently the Casadesus concerts have included a talented third member, son Jean, who first appeared with his parents in the Bach *Concerto in C Arranged for Three Pianos and Orchestra* in 1950. Jean was on his own in a Carnegie recital the following year.

Claudio Arrau, cool, distant, romantically handsome, came to the United States in November of 1923 from his native Chile by way of a prize-studded European career. A prodigy who gave his first concert at five and his formal Berlin début at eleven, Arrau has an enor-

mously live repertoire, with accents mainly—but not solely—in Beethoven and Bach, whose entire piano literature he has concertized several times over.

When speaking of Bach, one should also note a woman who excels in the works of this composer: Rosalyn Tureck. Although most widely known as a Bach specialist (her annual December program is a holiday treat), Miss Tureck is equally at home with Brahms and Beethoven or with modernists William Schuman and David Diamond. Miss Tureck brings to mind the many superb women pianists who have graced Carnegie's stage, including Ray Lev, Gina Bachauer, and Guiomar Novaes.

b. Robert Casadesus

a. Rosalyn Tureck

b. Claudio Arrau

95

Steinway Centennial: Finale, left to right—Ellen Ballon, Jacques Abram, Erno Balogh, Robert Casadesus, Abram Chasins, Dimitri Mitropoulos, Frank Mittler, Leonid Hambro, Jan Smeterlin, Alexander Uninsky, Muriel Kerr

Miss Novaes, a relaxed interpreter of Chopin and Schumann, won her audience's heart in 1954, when, after a glaring mistake, she stuck her tongue out at the keyboard and calmly proceeded with the piece.

Pianists are generally a witty lot. Most people know of the exchange between Kreisler and Rachmaninoff. Kreisler had a momentary lapse of memory during their joint recital. His bow poised, he whispered, "Where are we?" Rachmaninoff continued playing, blandly answered, "In Carnegie Hall." And Leonard Liebling tells a more edged story of Moriz Rosenthal and Godowsky at a Paderewski concert. During the intermission, Godowsky said, "Fine pianist." Rosenthal replied, "Yes, but he's no Paderewski." Fredric Fradkin was with Elman and Godowsky the night of Heifetz's debut. Following the boy's sensational performance the three men went out into the airless corridor behind their box. Elman wiped his brow, looked about, and mumbled, "It's awful hot in here." Godowsky quickly rejoined, "Not for pianists!"

There have been two spectacular piano programs in the last seventy years that must be mentioned. The first was held December 21, 1921, as a benefit for Moritz Moszkowski, German pianist-composer then penniless and ailing in Paris. Thirteen grand pianos were grouped onstage. Seated at them were fourteen grand pianists. Among them were Wilhelm Backhaus, Harold Bauer, Ossip Gabrilowitsch, Percy Grainger and Ernest Hutcheson (sharing a piano), Josef Lhevinne and Ernest Schelling. Walter Damrosch conducted, but said, "They don't need a conductor, they need a traffic cop."

The second "piano spectacular" was produced on October 19, 1953, to celebrate the one-hundredth anniversary of Steinway & Sons. Taking part in the program were no fewer than thirty-four pianists (alphabetically from Jacques Abram to Beveridge Webster), plus pianist-conductor Dimitri Mitropoulos and the Philharmonic (giving, incidentally, its 5,188th concert).

Ten smiling Steinway pianos were massed along the edge of the stage. At 8:45 the first platoon took their places and with the orchestra gave a spirited rendition of the "Star-Spangled Banner," as arranged by Josef Hofmann. Proceeding through Wagner, MacDowell, Prokofieff, Gould, Chopin, De Falla, and twenty-five pianists, the program ended in what was probably the most rousing finale in Carnegie Hall history: the pianos and the Philharmonic in a Morton Gould arrangement of Sousa's "Stars and Stripes Forever," a Steinway family favorite. Everyone took it *fortissimo* from A, and the black-tie audience roared its delight from start to atonal finish.

Among the pianists at this concert were several young men new to concert stage: Abram, Gary Graffman, Eugene List, William Masselos, Menahem Pressler. All are competent musicians, yet only three have gained broad

Van Cliburn
on his way to Carnegie stage

Van Cliburn with Kiril Kondrashin conducting

national recognition. The truth is that more fine performers are squeezed out of the concert field each year than America can really afford. The fact is obscured by the occasional artist who bursts on the scene through a rare combination of talent and timing. The most recent example is Harvey Lavan Cliburn, Jr.

Van Cliburn made his début with the Houston Symphony when he was twelve. He left Texas, his adopted state anyway, and came to Juilliard in New York to study with Rosina Lhevinne. In 1954, at twenty, he won the Edgar N. Leventritt Award and a Carnegie concert with the Philharmonic under Mitropoulos. This established Cliburn as the brightest hope of the year (or for the past four years, for that matter; no Leventritt Award was given between 1950 and 1954). However, high hopes can reap small rewards. Cliburn accepted a few concert dates and finally went overseas to enter the 1958 Tchaikovsky Piano Competition in Moscow. It is one in a long string of competitions that the young performer must enter to keep his name and his talent before

an apathetic public: The Queen Elisabeth of Belgium International Competition, the Michaels Memorial, the Gershwin Memorial, the Ferrucio Busoni contest, Musical Arts Piano Auditions, the Rachmaninoff Fund, the Naumburg Foundation, the Arthur Judson Foundation, the National Music Clubs, Geneva, Paris, London, Rome, New York—and Moscow.

Winning the post-Sputnik competition in Moscow took Van Cliburn off the musical treadmill. He had become an American secret weapon. On his return home he was given a ticker-tape parade down Broadway, the first United States musician to be so honored, a reception by the mayor, radio-TV interviews, and all manner of *brouhaha*. A special "return engagement" at Carnegie Hall was in order, this time with Kiril Kondrashin, who had conducted for Cliburn in Moscow, on the podium. The "talented newcomer" of 1954 "exceeded all expectations" in May, 1958, performing the Tchaikovsky *B-Flat Minor* and the Rachmaninoff *Third*. After the concert Cliburn

a. A standing ovation onstage

was besieged in the musicians' room by a mob of relatives, critics, friends, teachers, and newsmen.

The Cliburn concert was the highlight of the 1957-1958 season. Fame and a chance to earn a respectable income went to Van Cliburn partly through his own excellent musicianship, which was always there, and partly through the East-West ideological conflict, which had taken a new turn. But his success has done nothing to solve the difficult, usually impossible climb to recognition for the talented young men and women—many of them winners of competitions, too—who still stand waiting in the wings. The obvious answer is that each one ought to have his own Carnegie recital and garner his share of rave notices, too.

Carnegie Hall, of course, is the place to do it—but the price is high. A soloist must be able to raise enough cash or credit to meet the following expenses (as of January, 1959): *main hall rental* (the four walls) —$750; *liability insurance*—$40; *ushers and other nontechnical staff*—$225; *box-office fee*—$120; *stage crew—*

b.   . . . and backstage, too

$80; *spotlight—$25; spotlight operator—$25; ticket printing—$40; amplifier—$35; tape recording (for personal use)—$85; tape recording (for commercial use)—$250; stage seats (for an expected sellout)—$100.* This is roughly $1,500, but it doesn't cover everything. Still to come are the performance royalties for music still under copyright; a piano tuner; a page turner; the cost of "three-sheets," the large posters used outside the Hall; advertisements in the *Times*, the *Tribune*, and one or two key journals, as well as in the Carnegie Hall program itself; tuxedo rental or seamstress costs; free passes (deducted from the gross, hence an expense); *plus* photographs, press releases, cabs, cocktails, and all the nuisance incidentals that plague the performer.

Of course, it is possible to get the Hall with a $200 certified check and hope that box-office receipts will cover the remaining "curtain-raising" expenses. But this is risky. Even the chance of getting good notices can be wrecked if the night chosen for a début happens to be the night on which the Budapest String Quartet is appearing at Hunter, the Metropolitan is giving *Rigoletto*, the second-string critics are at a folk festival in Greenwich Village, the Calcutta Symphony is making its début at Lincoln Center, and friendly sponsors have left for a Franco-American gala in Boston. In a word, the odds against a young artist achieving prominence are so tremendous that the few who do—such recent Carnegie soloists as Leon Fleischer, Philippe Entremont, John Browning, Graffman, List, Cliburn, and Glenn Gould—have obviously earned it.

Considering the high costs and problems of performing, it is small wonder that genuine humor is missing in program after program. However, there have been some notable ex-

Glenn Gould warming up for a concert

a. Leon Fleisher

b. John Browning

c. Philippe Entremont

From left on sofa: Chalmers Clifton, John Erskine, Albert Stoessel; at double bass: Fabien Sevitsky, flanked by Harold Samuels, Josef Lhevinne; around piano: Paul Kochanski (with violin), Rudolph Ganz (at piano), Georges Barrère (with flute), Eugene Goossesn (leaning on piano); seated in center: Carl Friedbert, Lucrezia Bori, Yolanda Mero; with lawn mowers: Ernest Schelling, Harold Bauer; near piano, center: Felix Salmond, José Iturbi; with oboes: Olga Samaroff, Ernest Hutcheson; all conducted by John Philip Sousa

ceptions to this rule. One such occasion took place on December 30, 1929, when twenty-four leading artists donated their talents for a "Musicians' Gambol" to benefit the Edward MacDowell Association. A sparkling, packed house toted up $15,000, which the Association used to support the MacDowell Colony in Peterboro, New Hampshire. Among the creative people who had already enjoyed the freedom of the Colony were Willa Cather, Stephen Vincent Benét, Thornton Wilder, Elinor Wylie, and Aaron Copland. At the "Gambol" Mrs. MacDowell spoke of her late husband, then played the andante from his *Keltic* piano sonata. John Erskine, the president of Juilliard, also spoke. But the evening was to be a "gambol," and that's precisely how it started. Miss Lucrezia Bori sat on a Steinway (à la Helen Morgan) and warbled songs by De Falla and Granados, to the accompaniment of Ernest Schelling, popular conductor of children's concerts in the Hall. Walter Damrosch conducted Bach's *Concerto in C Arranged for Three Pianos and Orchestra*, with eight pianists alternating on the three pianos. Then John Philip Sousa stepped front and center to conduct Saint-Saëns's *The Carnival of the Animals* and Strauss's *Sinfonia Domestica*, for which

First row from left: Ernest Peixotto, Georges Barrère, John Philip Sousa, Josef Lhevinne. Second row on left: Carl Friedberg (slightly below), Fabien Sevitsky, John Erskine, Felix Salmond. Top Left: Rudolph Ganz. First row from right: José Iturbi, Harold Bauer, Walter Damrosch, Ernest Hutcheson, Paul Kochanski, Lucrezia Bori, Ernest Schelling. Second row, from right: Alfred Porchon, Yolanda Mero, Olga Samaroff

the guest stars played all manner of instruments and hardware in front of Ernest Peixotto's giant painting of a "follyphone."

Curiously enough, there were no violinists on the "gambol" program, an unfortunate omission. Although a variety of solo instruments has been heard here—from kazoo to koto—the piano and the violin have been dominant. Somewhat coincidentally, violinist (and ex-concertmaster) Adolf Brodsky was the first soloist in the Symphony Society's 1891 season and violinist (and ex-concertmaster) Joseph Fuchs was the last soloist of the Philharmonic-Symphony Society's last 1962 season at Carne-

gie. (Fuchs gave the premiere of Piston's *Concerto No. 2 for Violin and Orchestra* as a gesture of farewell; conductor Bernstein threw his baton to the audience during the final applause.)

One violinist whose career spanned the Hall's first seventy-one years was Fritz Kreisler. He first arrived—at age fourteen—in New York in November, 1888, for an auspicious Steinway Hall recital. The debut was shared by twenty-six-year-old Moriz Rosenthal. (A gifted pianist and master of the Chopin repertoire, Rosenthal had a brilliant career both here and in Europe and was honored with a jubilee pro-

Fritz Kreisler

gram in Carnegie Hall in 1938. No less a person than Eleanor Roosevelt, then First Lady, headed the anniversary committee.) Kreisler—like Fuchs, Menuhin, Stern, and others—was from a musical family; Vienna's leading chemist and its chief of police were among those who dropped by the house to play chamber music with Kreisler *père*, a fine 'cellist as well as a doctor.

Kreisler had no peer, when he was in his prime. Among his assets was a phenomenal memory; he once explained, "When I memorize, it is as if I engraved the music on a disc in my mind. . . . That disc will reproduce its record for years." (Once, arriving in London for a concert rehearsal and discovering his violin had not yet arrived, he called for a piano and played his part of the Mendelssohn *Violin Concerto* from memory.) The toughness of that memory was most dramatically revealed following his 1941 accident, when he was struck by an auto three blocks from Carnegie Hall at Fifty-seventh Street and Madison Avenue. He suffered a strange amnesia (re-

portedly he forgot all languages except Latin and Greek!) and for a while was very close to death. When he finally took up the violin again several months later, the virtuosity in his mind and his hands was revealed as unimpaired.

During his great years he could command $3,000 for a brief guest appearance. But he brought not just brilliant musicianship to the audience; he also brought an aura of romance and legend as well. He changed nationalities three times, had suffered wounds in combat, was known among musicians as an expert cardplayer, and played at one time or another the finest violins in the world: a Thir, a three-quarter Amati, a Gand & Bernardel (with his name inscribed in gold on the ribs, Kreisler's reward for winning the Premiere Grand Prix de Rome at the Paris Conservatoire), a Grancino, a Gagliano, a Guarneri del Gesù (vintage 1737), and a Stradivarius. From each he drew some of the finest sounds in the history of the violin art.

In his late sixties and beginning to tire,

a. Jascha Heifetz

b. David Oistrakh

c. Nathan Milstein

a. Joseph Szigeti

b. Adolph Busch

Fritz Kreisler dropped out of the musical life. He remained in seclusion from the end of World War II until his death, January 29, 1962.

As with any other instrument, the violin also encourages partisanship. Kreisler was not the sole favorite. In fact, another prodigy—sixteen-year-old Jascha Heifetz—had an extraordinary début in the Hall on October 27, 1917. It was a significant date: during the day the AEF fired its first shots of World War I (doughboys sent the shell case of the first round back to President Wilson) and marked the temporary —and in some cases final—eclipse of many Austro-German artists, including Kreisler. The Heifetz star rose quickly; his succeeding concerts earned reviews as glowing with superlatives as did Richard Aldrich's review in the *Times* of October 28. It praised the boy's "tone of power, smoothness and roundness, of searching expressiveness, of subtle modulation in power and color. His bowing is of rare elasticity and vigor...."

In World War I, Russian artists such as Heifetz had the edge on audience exposure; after the Armistice, they built continued acceptance of their training and talent. But World War II was not that congenial. A case in point is David Oistrakh. Throughout the thirties, Oistrakh was a celebrated soloist in Eastern Europe and a Queen Elisabeth of Belgium prizewinner (1937). During the forties he remained in the Soviet Union; but at war's end he extended his travels to Western Europe and as far east as Japan. Finally, on November 20, 1955, following the Geneva four-power summit conference, Oistrakh arrived for his American début in Carnegie Hall and lived up to all expectations. Seven years later, during another cold war thaw, David's talented violinist son Igor stepped onto the Carnegie stage for his first view of an American audience.

George Rabin has been a violinist with the New York Philharmonic for many years, a well beloved member of the section. Though not as famous as David Oistrakh by any means, he does share with the Russian the parental joy of having a son who is a violin virtuoso. Young Michael Rabin had his debut in Carnegie with "his father's orchestra" in 1950. He was then fourteen. Michael has returned to

a. Gregor Piatigorsky

b. at the cello

the Hall annually ever since, establishing himself as a major contender for violin laurels for many years to come. By 1962, Rabin had also earned another title of sorts: "The most traveled musician of his generation," having completed ten cross-country tours of the United States, plus many tours abroad. For many Europeans, Rabin is proof that young American artists are not only excellent—they are consistently so in visit after visit.

The roster of great string musicians who have appeared in Carnegie Hall is rich with the genius of the past seventy years. At times, concertgoers have had the rare privilege of hearing trios of matchless personnel: the Milstein-Piatigorsky-Horowitz trio of 1931 or the Stern-Rose-Istomin trio of 1962. And whether they remain as recitalists or—as did Thomas, Damrosch, Koussevitzky, Wallenstein, Toscanini, and others—go on to conducting, the Hall and its auditors have been continually enriched. There is one name, however, which stands for high achievement both in recital and on the podium: Pablo Casals.

When Carnegie Hall opened in 1891, Casals, then fifteen, was making his début as a 'cellist 2,000 miles away in Barcelona. He thereafter pursued his art wherever it led him—in café quartets, casino orchestras, theaters, opera houses, and symphony halls. In 1899 he was hailed as a great talent after performing Lalo's 'Cello Concerto in Paris. In 1901-1902, the first of many American tours brought the art of Pablo Casals to an even wider audience.

Casals' particular contribution was to show the 'cello as being as rich and as versatile as the violin, with very nearly the same three-octave range. Casals' style of playing is akin to a violinist's: the fingers, for example, do not anticipate extension but remain in normal playing postures until the moment of attack (the "lashing out") down the fingerboard; after the attack, the finger immediately returns to its next, more favorable position. Such a style has freed 'cellists to explore the virtuoso literature of Bach, Mozart, Brahms, Beethoven, and Schubert in particular. It also encouraged modern composers (Enesco, Villa-Lobos, De

Pablo Casals

Falla) to think of the 'cello as a solo instrument with new potential.

Casals was back after World War I as conductor as well as soloist, appearing with the New York Symphony in both Carnegie and Aeolian halls. He had already founded the excellent Casals Orchestra in Barcelona. But he abandoned everything years later when Franco buried the republic in civil war. Casals' exile from Spain to France (in the border town of Prades) and finally to Puerto Rico is well known, as is his gradual return to public life, via the United Nations General Assembly and the White House. Then, on June 21 and 22, 1962, Pablo Casals returned to Carnegie Hall after nearly a forty-year absence. The occasion was the presentation of the First Carnegie Hall Award "for distinguished service to the arts and humanity," sponsored by the Carnegie Hall Society. Casals brought the orchestra of the Festival Casals (an annual event in San Juan, Puerto Rico) to the Hall, augmented by the Cleveland Orchestra Chorus. On the 21st, Casals was given the award by White House arts consultant August Heckscher and he made a short speech on the value of Carnegie Hall to America and the world. (Among those applauding was his good friend and concert companion, Queen Elisabeth of Belgium.) The following night Casals conducted the Festival Orchestra and the Cleveland Chorus in his own *El Pesebre* (The Manger) oratorio. Although eighty-five years old and seated in a swivel chair on the podium, Casals was vigorous where vigor was demanded and often rose from the chair to draw the

a. Pablo Casals conducting

b. From left: Rudolf Serkin, Mieczyslaw Horszowski, Casals and Eugene Istomin

c. Isaac Stern and his accompanist Alexander Zalken rehearsing at Carnegie Hall for an appearance there that evening

109

b. Clara, Wally, Arturo Toscanini

a. Mme. Alma Gluck Zimbalist and Efrem, Jr.

c. Sigrid Onegin and Fritz Peter

desired crescendo from the orchestra. The performance over, the audience rose and applauded for nine minutes. Casals, visibly moved, took six stage bows, then shook hands and kissed those who crowded about him on the stage.

The Casals appearance in June, 1962, after the regular season had ended, proved beyond a doubt that the departure of the Philharmonic, the Boston, the Philadelphia and other orchestras for Lincoln Center the following season would not mean the boarding up of Carnegie Hall. And the achievement of keeping Carnegie Hall a "vital center" of great art belongs to another string virtuoso, violinist Isaac Stern.

In the late 1950s, Robert Simon, Jr., complained of the losses Carnegie Hall was piling

d. Igor Markevitch and Olege

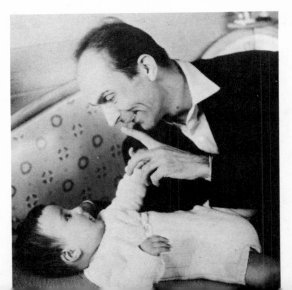

a. Pierre Monteux and Mme. Monteux

b. Igor and David Oistrakh

c. Dean David, Dean, Sieglinde Crane

d. Jascha Heifetz and Jay

f. Walter Gieseking and granddaughter

e. Irina, Sergei, Tatiana Rachmaninoff

Igor Stravinsky tasting his wife's famous chicken soup under her watchful eye

up for his real estate syndicate and decided to tear it down. A great hue and cry was raised against the move, but Simon seemed firm. At first, a red skyscraper was to have been built on the site, but luckily that idea was abandoned. Then Simon planned merely to raze the Hall for a parking lot, and he set about evicting tenants and curbing all activities in the famous old building. Committees of every size and interest were formed to save the Hall. Tenants' committees sprang up in the main building and in the adjacent Rembrandt Building; the Telemann Society was on the move; and a trio was formed from yet another camp: composer Deems Taylor, Hall manager John Totten, and Sidney Kaye (hospodar of the

Russian Tea Room, afterconcert meeting place just a few steps from the Hall itself). From the stage Dame Myra Hess, Leopold Stokowski, Leonard Bernstein, and many other artists began, interrupted, or ended their programs with a plea to the audience for help. One wag suggested in the *Times* that the Soviet Union should buy the Hall and donate it to New York as a form of foreign aid.

In the midst of all this feverish—but fruitless—activity, Isaac Stern assumed leadership of a Citizens Committee to Save Carnegie Hall. With the same zest and keen intelligence with which he approaches his music, Stern attacked this problem, also. He confronted Mayor Wagner with a plan of action which made financial, as well as political, sense. Stern and the Mayor carried the idea to Governor Nelson Rockefeller, who drafted enabling legislation. It was passed by the state legislature just prior to Simon's effective deadline. The formula: The state allowed the city to condemn the privately owned building and then assume its operation. Wagner agreed next to the purchase price of $5,000,000. Step three was the handing over of the Hall to a private, nonprofit Carnegie Hall Corporation (Isaac Stern, President) which would carry out the actual maintenance, operations, and debt service of the property.

It's probably typical of New York that this success story was carried out by a non-New Yorker. Isaac Stern was born in the Ukrainian farm center of Kremenets, but came to America as an infant, his family settling in San Francisco. He was eleven when he had his debut with Pierre Monteux and the San Francisco Symphony in 1931. Six years later he was in Town Hall and received mixed notices from the New York press. Another six years passed, involving world tours and better notices, before he appeared in Carnegie Hall in 1943. For that concert the critics were unanimous in their praise.

If there is any artist who might typify all those who have appeared at Carnegie, it could well be Stern. He is a hard worker who maintains his exceptional level of achievement by constant study and practice. Above all, he exudes a comforting, homely warmth, which is also typical of the real virtuoso. When Stern plays—either at rehearsal or in concert—the vastness of Carnegie Hall is reduced to the comfort of one's living room. Despite world fame and a constant spotlight, Stern—indeed, all the fine artists who have appeared here—prefers to remain life-sized. Carnegie Hall, with its unimpeded sightlines and intimate acoustics, has always promoted this warm, personal relationship between performer and audience.

Artur Rubinstein, Blanche Thebom, Marian Anderson and Mme. Rubinstein (back to camera)

6 * Intermission Stroll

A SCHOOL of social theory believes that civilization is advanced not by hard work or virtuoso achievements, but through play. By his genius for fun, by his explosion of gaiety, man shapes his cultural destiny.

When Carnegie Hall was built in 1891, the country expressed its rosy self-confidence in many ways. Whitcomb Judson invented the zipper and Dr. James Naismith originated basketball. "Plugger Bill" Martin won the first international six-day bike race ever held in this country. Edison patented the movie camera and George Hale made sun photography possible by inventing the spectroheliograph. Charles Hoyt's San Francisco farce, *A Trip to Chinatown*, ran for a record 650 performances and featured A. J. Libby in that all-time favorite "After the Ball Is Over."

In its buildings this easygoing, free-spending age enjoyed itself, too. It liked surprises in its pseudo-palazzos: dens hidden by innocent red brocades, wrought-iron fence tops of legendary beasts, occult flowers in dollhouse conservatories, satyrs and angels, lambs and lions, a never-never land of terracotta, marble, and bronze. Bits of the Levant, a hint of the Moors, essence of China, suggestions of France, the voluptuousness of baroque Italy were built into the homes and public places. Hunt and George B. Post were reincarnating Europe, stone by stone, in the fashionable areas of New York. A Fifth Avenue stroller could gaze for half an hour on any single château and never see the same thing twice. What he did see was not always brilliant, but it was genuinely delightful nevertheless.

Hence, when Tuthill and Hunt worked out the details of Carnegie Hall, a building which would serve the entertainment-seekers of the age, they enlisted the aid of a small army of molders and sculptors, artisans of the Land of Alice. These workmen contributed sprays of acanthus, vine-circled antique rosettes, Roman consoles, egg-and-dart moldings, long panels of fruit and flowers, fluting and foliation, all of it expressing a genial courtship of nature.

The ornamentation bedecking Carnegie Hall is not priceless art. Much of it is admittedly pedestrian, yet it contributes to the sense of play which this great hall embodies.

The twentieth century has been, in this respect, somewhat disappointing. But the remnants of yesterday's granite menagerie exist, like the whooping crane, on the very edge of extinction, preserved only by our vague sense of duty toward them, rather than our joy of being among them.

The Carnegie concertgoer has, therefore, a special treat in store. A casual intermission stroll through the halls and up the stairs will reveal to the sharp eye a world of symmetry and detail, of ordered design, of those small delights that make up the good laughter of civilization.

Playhouse: composite capital of Corinthian acanthus leaves, Roman egg-and-dart molding, Ionic volute with rosettes; fluting on upper third of shaft, rest is smooth

a. Composite pilaster. Volutes, acanthus leaves, bracket scrolls, egg-and-dart moldings, dentils, laurel wreath and sprays, band of rinceaux.

b. Note decoration of coffered ceiling beams. Renaissance ornament around door.

a. Playhouse, detail of balcony balustrade: top molding is egg-and-dart over antique Greek details; cherubs hold French Renaissance strapwork tablet; behind and underfoot are oak-and-laurel festoons and molding; a French grotesque is below tablet; base molding is German Renaissance evolute-spiral ("the running wave")

b. West hallway, street level, corbel at archway: doubly-curved scroll faced with acanthus; egg-and-dart, egg-and-leaf, bead-and-reel moldings

117

(Opposite) Pilaster panel of Main Hall proscenium; baroque cherub entwined in acanthus vine (detail)

b. Theater, upstairs lounge (formerly the balcony): Doric architrave, coffered beams; unsuccessful capital of inverted acanthus and rosettes supports plain abacus

a. Playhouse: balcony supported by recumbent composite bracket. Romanesque: convex circular panel has classic leaves radiating from central cartouche.

c. Recital Hall architrave: egg-and-dart molding; light in inverted laurel wreath

a. Cast bronze decorated candelabrum embellished with classical variant moldings; enfoliated oblong panel; shaft is partially fluted, has foliated panel at arm's height; exposed iron screwheads

Newel posts showing how ornament often denoted social strata; (Below, left) Dull post, exposed hardware, wrought iron railing, wooden banister, lower to upper balcony; (Below) Richly ornamented post from stairs, parquet to first tier

a. Slimmer newel post with prosaic decoration, second tier to family circle

b. Close-up of composite pilaster (page 116)

c. Elaborate corner treatment: intersecting cornices with double-curved scrolls faced with acanthus, rosettes, egg-and-dart, bead-and-reel, leaf molding; rectangular plaque enclosing garland motif with flying ribbons

7 * Theater

LAWRENCE Barrett, Edwin Booth, Helena Modjeska, Mlle. Sarah Bernhardt, and manager Henry E. Abbey were the prominent names in the world of theater when Franklin Haven Sargent, a Harvard professor of Greek and elocution, left the Elysium of the Yard for the Acheron of Times Square in 1882. The Mallory brothers (the Reverend George S. and Marshall H.) hired Sargent to tutor a flock of ingenues backstage at their Madison Square theater. Here Sargent fell in with a company of theater geniuses: Steele MacKaye, actor-playwright-director, who designed the Madison's revolutionary mechanical stage; Henry C. De Mille, resident play reader—at $1,500 a year—and playwright—at $1,000 per play if it ran 200 nights; the remarkable Frohmans—Charles, Daniel, and Gustave; and the Frohmans' fellow San Franciscan, twenty-nine-year-old David Belasco. Among the stars then playing the Madison were Annie Russell, Cora Tanner, and Henry Miller.

In 1884 Sargent conceived the idea of a formal school for young actors on the European model. By then he had won the confidence and respect of MacKaye and Gustave Frohman. With each man reportedly investing $40,000, they left the Mallorys and founded the Lyceum Theatre School in the old Lyceum Theatre building at Twenty-third Street and Fourth Avenue. At this time MacKaye and his friend, Thomas A. Edison, turned the Lyceum Theatre into New York's first all-electric playhouse.

Sargent, MacKaye, and Frohman had a ten-year lease and high hopes. Hopes were quickly fulfilled, when, between October and May of their first season, they received "eight to ten applicants a day." The school prospered and attracted the attention of Lawrence Barrett. With associate Edwin Booth, Barrett dominated the Shakespearean repertoire. He engaged Sargent's class of one hundred for his production of *Julius Caesar* in January, 1885.

Sargent brought in his only competitor, Charles Frohman (floundering with a rival Empire Theatre School) and Henry C. De Mille. De Mille suggested to Sargent that the school's name be changed (for the fourth time) to the American Academy of Dramatic Arts, the name that has lasted until today.

The Academy soon grew out of its cramped Lyceum quarters and moved in 1892 to the Berkeley Lyceum Theatre uptown at Forty-fourth Street and Fifth Avenue.

The year before, 1891, the great Barrett died and Booth retired to a sickbed. It was also the year Carnegie Hall was opened, including its fair-sized basement auditorium, designed for lectures and chamber music. By 1896, however, the Music Hall Company had acquired an adjoining stable, knocked it down, and had raised a sixteen-story tower called its lateral building, the highest tower in a three-square-mile area at that time. In the bowels of the main building, next to the Lyceum (the basement auditorium), other improvements were made; the old kitchen, freezers, and serving rooms, rusted with disuse, were pulled out and new steam boilers and dynamos went in. Sar-

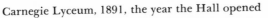

Carnegie Lyceum, 1891, the year the Hall opened

b. Dimmer board, offstage

a. Backstage wall, showing effects of modernization

gent, on the lookout for bigger quarters, supervised some of the Carnegie renovation, watched the modest Lyceum be widened, deepened, and take on added storage and dressing-room space. Having learned the lessons of MacKaye and Edison, Sargent cut into the old-era ornament to install the new-era electrical wiring. In the dusty corners of this little theater is dramatic evidence of the most significant moment in the history of modern stagecraft: the arrival of electric lights.

Sargent's Academy took over the Lyceum and a good deal of the rest of Carnegie, too. The two top floors of the lateral building housed the Academy's offices; the next floor down had two enormous rehearsal rooms; on the eighth floor, which meets the main building's sixth floor at a small landing, were suites of classrooms; several rooms of the second floor, above the Art Gallery, were also the Academy's.

Sargent was now director of a large and important enterprise, which he supervised from his tower suite. ("In every direction the view was boundless," wrote an enchanted visitor with unwitting perception.) His pronouncements upon native art were soberly reported, as in this paragraph from the *Sun:* "Probably the most serious obstacle to the advancement of the stage applicant in America is self-consciousness. Our nerve-exciting climate, and the character of our institutions, and the manner in which women are treated in this country make the applicant often very self-conscious for a long time, and until that self-consciousness is dropped off, like a garment, their real spontaneous nature doesn't appear...." Further along in this interview he flatly declared, "The Irish have the most dramatic talent."

William Birney of the Washington *Post,* after seeing a company of Academy students perform, concluded that "The Academy is a

a. Franklin Haven Sargent, founder of the American Academy of Dramatic Arts

b. Daniel Frohman with group which includes (from left) Nicholas Murray Butler and Hazel and Eleanor Dawn (with corsages)

professional training school superior in its methods to most schools of law or medicine." Certainly its faculty was eminently competent: Mme. Giulia Valda (opera), Edwin Belknap (pantomime), William Buckland (makeup), David Belasco (rehearsal methods), Charles Frohman (who inaugurated a revolutionary work-study plan for penniless students), Charles Jehlinger ("Mr. Jelly"; acting; later succeeded Sargent as director), and Wellington Putname (rhetoric; "His method was simple," recalls former student Cecil B. De Mille; "It was drill!"). Guest lecturers included Brander Matthews, Joseph Jefferson, John Drew, Bronson Howard, George Pierce Baker, May Robson, and other leading theater

a. Charles ("Jehli") Jehlinger

b. David Belasco

c. Charles Frohman on *Lusitania,* 1915

a. Agnes Moorehead

b. Hume Cronyn

c. Spencer Tracy

personalities. Student productions were as exciting as most offerings of the White Way farther downtown; in addition, they introduced to American audiences new plays by Gerhart Hauptman *(Lonely Lives),* Shaw *(The Man of Destiny),* Björnstjerne Björnson *(Pastor Sang),* Ibsen *(The Pillars of Society),* and Maeterlinck *(The Intruder).* The Academy also began a Children's Theater under Belasco's guidance. ("He had the spirit of fun that children love," wrote Cecil De Mille, "and with it the rarer gift of taking children seriously, treating them as persons. . . .")

Despite Sargent's gloomy view of "applicants," they came to his Academy in goodly numbers. The roster of graduates contains some of the most honored names in theater: Spencer Tracy, Agnes Moorhead, Edward G. Robinson, Hume Cronyn, Betty Field, Garson Kanin, Anne Bancroft, Jennifer Jones, and Rosalind Russell. All trudged up and down the marble steps to and from class, studied makeup in the stuffy backstage area, curled up in the dark, warm balcony of the main hall to hear a Philharmonic rehearsal, and swapped pointers with students of other schools

d. Anne Bancroft

e. Tom Poston

f. Garson Kanin

Ellen Terry leaving for America, 1911

of drama also housed in Carnegie Hall (Lucy Feagin School, Mary Stuart's, Elizabeth Grimball's). They would huddle in the Lyceum balcony to watch rehearsals of a Broadway play (the Lyceum was regarded as one of the city's better rehearsal halls), or during the forties would go next door and meet students from the Art Students League.

A note about "next door." When Robert Simon, Sr., added a row of stores on the Seventh Avenue side of the Hall, one of these was leased to Mort Friedlander for his Carnegie Hall Pharmacy. One day an enterprising young man named Art Green sublet the basement storeroom from Mort and opened a tiny luncheonette. Art's salesmanship soon drew

students, friends, and jobless actors, who sat and sipped nepenthe by the hour. Green cleverly jammed in nine phone booths, symbol of hope to every struggling artist. (A sign advertised: "Would You Believe It? Phone Messages and Telegrams Taken For You For Only $1.50 A Month.") Academy students discovered a "secret" entrance that connected their locker rooms with this lively subemporium and they made good use of it. Until the arrival of the present Nedick's, the Carnegie Hall Pharmacy contributed warmth and a certain exhilaration to the local community of young artists.

Although the American Academy of Dramatic Arts was the principal theater tenant in

Sarah Bernhardt and Martin Beck

Carnegie Hall for sixty years, there have been many important theatrical events given upstairs in the main hall, too. Among the first stars to appear was Mlle. Sarah Bernhardt in a program of readings, April, 1892. (Twelve years earlier, when Henry Abbey introduced her to this country, New York ecclesiastics called her "the European courtesan who has come to ruin the morals of the American people.") Joseph Jefferson, Matthews, Twain and others lectured or gave readings in the main hall, Chapter Hall, Recital Hall, and the Lyceum. Ellen Terry rented the Hall in 1910 for a one-woman show. In later years Ingrid Bergman read *Joan of Lorraine* and the First Drama Quartet read *Don Juan in Hell.* These were professionals, but nonprofessionals also found Carnegie to be a congenial playhouse.

From the time of the 1896 renovation until the 1960 renovation, the Lyceum had been popular with community groups of all kinds. Early programs list performances by La Ci-

gale Society, the Eclectic Medical Society, the Inner Seal Association, the Merrymakers, and the Philomel Choral Society. With more regularity and frequently more success appeared the productions of the Amateur Comedy Club, founded in 1884 by a septet of true-bloods in search of good-fellowship and creative expression. (This search happily continues in a refurbished carriage house at Sniffen Court and Thirty-sixth Street.) Lawyers, doctors, publishers, and financiers let their hair down (or up, as the occasion demanded) to produce such operas as *The Ghost of Jerry Blunder, Foiled Again (or The Sob of the Painted Woman), The Bathroom Door, Carrot & Co. Vs. The Guano Association,* and *Bluebeard in Bologna.* Attendance was by invitation only, a clever way of protecting the general public. The ACC moved from the Berkeley Lyceum to Carnegie in 1895, opening with *7-20-8 (or Casting the Boomerang), a Comedy of To-Day in Four Acts,* by Augustin Daly. (At this time

Lotte Lenya

John Drew and Ada Rehan were in the stock company at Daly's Theatre, Broadway.) The Club began as an all-male enterprise, but quickly added bylaws to bring in ladies (but only as "associate members," to be sure). One of the founders, piano maker Theodore Steinway, acted with and then married associate member Ruth Davis, proving that footlights and grease paint, like hearts and flowers, are also the stuff of love.

In recent years, the Lyceum has been known as the Carnegie Playhouse. The principal lessee was an exhibitor of 16mm film classics (*The*

a. Early performance of Amateur Comedy Club on Carnegie Lyceum stage

b. A scene from *Greater than the Law*

a. Ruth Davis as Noeline

b. Theodore Steinway as André

134

Great Train Robbery, Tillie's Punctured Romance, etc.), which is rather grim justice: when the Lyceum opened as a theater in 1896, the big event in New York was a series of short films shown at Koster & Bial's Music Hall—an umbrella dance, a risqué skirt dance, two comedians boxing—produced by Thomas Edison and W. K. L. Dickson. ("Wonderfully real and singularly exhilarating," said the awed *Times.*) During the 1960 renovation, the Playhouse was done over as a true motion picture theater and renamed Carnegie Hall Cinema. Foreign art films are its specialty.

However, before the transformation into the Cinema, the Playhouse was also a haven for off-Broadway dramatists who wanted to do something different. It was not, unfortunately, the most pleasant hall in town: the Simon management allowed the Playhouse to deteriorate after the American Academy moved out; broken seats were not replaced; lighting was in bad repair; dirt and refuse lay piled in the once-cozy corners. An insidious arrangement of leasing, subleasing, and sub-subleasing

The Playhouse

b. Earlier photograph of Miss Hayden

a. Theresa Hayden in rehearsal

Miss Hayden coaches Michael Shillo and (right) Eva Stern in theater lounge

rotted the integrity of this historic auditorium. But in an age when theaters of every description have been converted into television studios or supermarkets, the mere existence of the Playhouse was acknowledged with gratitude by stage experimentalists. One such group appeared in March, 1960, to present Mrs. Aldyth Morris's exotic "Chinese" play, *The Secret Concubine*. Directing it was Miss Terese Hayden, who was last on the Playhouse stage in 1941 costarring with Kirk Douglas in a production by the senior class of the Academy. The Morris play was mounted by Miss Hayden, Elaine Aiken, and Ira J. Bilowit, whose Unicorn Productions operated out of a Forty-sixth Street basement.

Rehearsals were held upstairs in a large foyer that was once the balcony. (As an indication of the depth of the theater, this foyer is now the basement floor of a paperback bookstore that fronts on Fifty-seventh Street, while the rear wall of the stage is under the first row of seats of the long main hall parquet.) The small *Concubine* company of fifteen spread out in the existing makeup rooms; leading players Eva Stern, Myra Carter, and Adelaide Klein shared a lean-to in the wings, small and hot as a telephone booth. The critics reviewed the little enterprise with customary kindness; said Brooks Atkinson of the *Times*, "Under Terese Hayden's direction, *The Secret Concubine* is produced with taste.

a. Myra Carter and Eva Stern in makeshift dressing room

b. Everyone is briefed in the technical rehearsal

Wolfgang Roth's scenery . . . is admirable . . . interesting and useful. The costumes, too, have . . . simplicity and richness." Michael Shillo, the male lead, formerly a member of Israel's famed Kameri Theatre and Habima companies, was singled out as an actor with "the voice and the technique to play a character who is bigger than life."

The Secret Concubine was the last production in the Carnegie Playhouse. Since then the Hall has been saved; the theater, however, is converted. Yet, like the other auditoriums in this building, the Carnegie Hall Cinema is still an antique. Which is not a criticism. As Archibald MacLeish has written: "There is nothing worse for our trade than to be in style."

First Drama Quartet backstage: Charles Boyer, Charles Laughton, Sir Cedric Hardwicke, Agnes Moorehead

8 * Jazz

JIMMIE MARSHALL used to run a hotel and club on West Fifty-third Street, near Sixth Avenue. In pre-World War I days, Marshall's was the gathering place of such Negro stars as Bert Williams ("the whole nation is ruled by syncopation"), composer J. Rosamond Johnson, Ford Dabney, and James Reese Europe. Some say that jazz hit New York first in 1903 in Marshall's lively hotel. However, white New Yorkers really heard the new music first in 1912, when Jim Europe and 125 Negro musicians rented Carnegie Hall for the first of several concerts by the "Clef Club." (Before the Club disbanded in the twenties it numbered such fine musicians as singer-bandleader Noble Sissle, pianist Eubie Blake, and others.) This Clef Club concert was given five years before the Original Dixieland Jass Band opened in Reisenweber's Café two blocks north of Carnegie Hall. Although the 1917 ODJB event is often noted as the début of "jass" in New York, it was only the début of the word itself (later changed to "jazz"). The Clef Club actually brought this music to New York attention first a good five years earlier.

The Clef Club's leader, Jim Europe, was an Army lieutenant in World War I. He led the 369th Regimental Band (the Hellfighters) to the Continent in 1919 and gave Europeans their first hearing of jazz.

In 1912, while the Clef Club was swinging in Carnegie, an Alabama coronet player named William Christopher Handy reworked "Mr. Crump," a campaign song for Mayor Edward Hull "Boss" Crump. The new title:

"Memphis Blues." It was the first written blues in jazz literature, soon to be followed by "St. Louis Blues," "Yellow Dog Blues," "Beale Street," and others.

Handy and his family came to New York in the twenties and settled permanently. He became a leading force in the jazz world, introducing and befriending many men and women whose gift for music was their only possession. This was a roaring period for jazz. Its new rhythms and melodies were the fabric of many Broadway hits and of the first "talkie," Al Jolson's *The Jazz Singer*.

The arrival of W. C. Handy, his wife, three daughters, and son in Carnegie Hall for their historic program was a peak in jazz music's long uphill battle for acceptance by the white majority. Handy picked top people for his program at the Hall. Among them was a short, round, riotously funny young butterball named Thomas "Fats" Waller. Barely twenty-four at the time, Fats already had a reputation uptown in Harlem and in Negro clubs around the country. James P. Johnson had taken him on as a student years before; he had worked with the Fletcher Henderson and Erskine Tate bands; and he had been Bessie Smith's accompanist during her great 1926 tour. In New York he was famous mainly for his sly improvisations on the Lincoln Theatre's giant Wurlitzer organ. (Fats was brought up on Bach, whose organ music he continually explored.) His featured appearance at Carnegie Hall, under the Handy aegis, was his first "downtown" success. It established his repu-

Carnegie Hall   Program

CARNEGIE HALL
Friday Evening, April 27th, 1928.

W. C. Handy's Orchestra and Jubilee Singers

PROGRAM
PROLOGUE
a. "The Birth of Jazz".......Handy-Smith-Troy
b. "The Memphis Blues".................Handy

SPIRITUALS—ARR. HANDY
1—a. "Steal Away To Jesus"
   b. "Wheel In A Wheel"
   c. "I've Heard of a City Called Heaven"
     Orchestra and Chorus

BLUES
2—a. "Yellow Dog Blues".................Handy
   b. "St. Louis Blues"...................Handy
    Solo-Mezzo Soprano Katherine Handy
   c. "Beale Street Blues".................Handy

PLANTATION SONGS
3—a. "Golden Slippers".........James A. Bland
   b. "Carry Me Back To Old Virginny"
                James A. Bland
    Tenor Solo—George E. Jackson
   c. "My Old Virginia Home"..Rucker & Lofton
    Tenor Solo—Russell Smith

SPIRITUALS—ARR. HANDY
4—a. "I'm Drinking From A Fountain"
   b. "Give Me Jesus"
     Orchestra and Chorus

WORK SONGS—ARR. HANDY
5—a. "Goin' To See My Sarah"
   b. "Joe Jacobs"
     Orchestra and Male Voices

PIANO SOLO
6—a. "Bamboula" ....Coleridge-Taylor
   b. "Juba Dance" ....Nathaniel Dett
     Sidney Brown

SPIRITUALS Arr. J. Rosamond Johnson
7—a. "Didn't My Lord Deliver Daniel"
   b. "O Wasn't Dat A Wide River"
   c. "Witness For My Lord"
    J. Rosamond Johnson and Taylor Gordon

CHARACTER SONGS
8—a. "The Unbeliever",
         Bert Williams-Smith-Bryan
   b. "Wouldn't That Be A Dream"
                Hogan-Jordan
    Tom Fletcher
  Accompanist, Bernardin Brown
    Intermission
    Part Two

9—Cake Walk........Featuring Mme. Robinson
   a. "Dark Town Is Out Tonight"
              Will Marion Cook
   b. "Exhortation" ....Will Marion Cook
     Male Voices

NEGRO RHAPSODY
10—a. "Yamekraw"............James P. Johnson
     Orchestra
   Piano—Thomas (Fats) Waller

SOPRANO SOLO
11—a. "Spring Had Come" (Hiawatha),
              Coleridge Taylor
   b. "Hear The Lamb A-Cryin' "..H. T. Burleigh
   c. "Joshua Fit De Battle of Jericho",
             Arr. Lawrence Brown
    Minnie Brown
  Accompanist—Andrades Lindsey

XYLOPHONE SOLO
12—"Maple Leaf Rag"...............Scott Joplin
    W. C. Handy, Jr.

SOPRANO SOLO
13—"Africa" ....Ford Dabney
    Josephine Hall

J. ROSAMOND JOHNSON
14—a. "African Drum Dance" No. 1,
         J. Rosamond Johnson
    Piano Solo
   b. "Under The Bamboo Tree",
         J. Rosamond Johnson
    Baritone Solo

JAZZ FINALE
15 a. "Shimmy Like My Sister Kate",
         Clarence Williams
    Clarence Williams
   b. "I Ain't Got Nobody"....Spencer Williams
     Male Voices
   c. "I'm Feelin' Devilish"......Maceo Pinkard
     Orchestra
   d. "St. Louis Blues"...................Handy
    Organ Solo—Thomas (Fats) Waller
    Orchestra and Chorus

STEINWAY PIANO USED

Management: Robert Clairmont

b. Elizabeth, Lucile, Katherine and Mrs. W. C. Handy

"Fats"

tation as a master of rent-party piano, the equal of such men as James P. Johnson, Willie "The Lion" Smith, and Charles Luckeyeth Roberts. Just before his death in 1943, Fats returned to Carnegie for his own concert. In April, 1944, a "Tribute to Fats" brought to the Carnegie stage Mezz Mezzrow, Art Hodes, Pops Foster, Duke Ellington, Count Basie, Teddy Wilson, Bill Robinson, Billie Holiday, Paul Draper (improvising to jazz), and comics Zero Mostel and Jimmy Savo.

The jazz omnibus program is now almost a cliché; yet several Carnegie programs of this type have made jazz history. One of the most significant was a 1938 concert titled "From Spirituals to Swing." Produced by an astute young critic-impresario, John Hammond, the program was dedicated to the Empress of the Blues, Bessie Smith. Bessie had been injured in an auto accident in Virginia the year before; she was rushed to the nearest hospital—which didn't admit Negroes. Before her friends could get her to a "colored" hospital, the first great jazz voice in history was forever silenced.

In honor of Bessie Smith a broad representation of Negro music was featured, from Sister Rosetta Tharpe (spirituals) to Count Basie (swing). "The producers of this concert ask

143

CARNEGIE HALL PROGRAM
SEASON 1941-1942
Wednesday Evening, January 14, at 8:30

Concert by
FATS WALLER
with Assisting Artists

•

THE PROGRAM

1. At the piano—THE SONGS OF FATS WALLER

In order to give Mr. Waller all possible liberty in selecting his material and in order to retain a maximum of spontaneity for his performance, no formal program has been arranged. In this, his first group of selections at the piano, he will play some of his own popular compositions. A list of the best known of them follows. He may be expected to play several of these items. Some of the best of Mr. Waller's popular songs (which are *not* included in this list) are not credited to him simply because he sold all rights to them to unscrupulous Tin Pan Alley authors.

1919 Squeeze Me	1931 I'm Crazy 'bout My Baby
1926 Senorita Mine	Heart of Stone
1927 I'm More Than Satisfied	Take It From Me
St. Louis Shuffle	Concentratin' on You
1928 Candied Sweets	The Iceman Lives in an
Willow Tree	Ice House
Got Myself Another Jockey	1932 Keepin' Out of Mischief Now
Now	Buddy
1929 Ain't Misbehavin'	If It Ain't Love
I've Got a Feelin' I'm Fallin'	Radio Poppa, Broadcastin'
Gone	Mamma
My Fate is in your Hands	When Gabriel Blows His
Zonky	Horn
Honeysuckle Rose	Lonesome Me
Black & Blue	Gotta Be, Gonna Be Mine
How Jazz was Born	Oh You Sweet Thing
Dixie Cinderella	Strange As It Seems
Sweet Savannah Sue	That Where the South Begins
Can't We Get Together	Angeline
Snakehip Dance	My Heart's at Ease
That Rhythm Man	Sheltered by Stars
Off-time	I Didn't Dream It Was Love
Why Am I Alone with No	Old Yazoo
One To Love	1933 Aintcha Glad
1930 Rollin' Down the River	Tall Timber
Blue Turning Grey over You	Sittin' Up Waitin' For You
Keep a Song in your Soul	Doin' What I Please
Little Brown Betty	I've Got You Where I
Prisoner of Love	Want You
	Handful of Keys
1934 Swing On Mississippi	1938 Inside This Heart of Mine
How Can You Fail Me	On Rainy Days
Piano Pranks	Hold My Hand
1935 Numb Fumblin'	I Got Love
1936 Smashin' Thirds	Bluer Than The Ocean Blues
Stealin' Apples	I'm Gonna Fall in Love
I Can See You All Over the	Cottage in the Rain
Place	What a Pretty Miss
The Panic Is On	Not There, Right Here
Sugar Rose	Moonlight Mood
1937 Our Love Was Meant To Be	The Spider and the Fly
Lost Love	Patty Cake, Patty Cake
Call the Plumber In	I Can't Forgive You
Crazy 'bout That Man of	1939 The Jitterbug Tree
Mine	1940 The Joint Is Jumpin'
The Short Trail Became a	Happy Feelin'
Long Trail	Stayin' at Home
Swingin' Hound	1941 All That Meat and No
Any Day the Sun Don't	Potatoes
Shine	Mamacita
Brother Ben	Blue Velvet
Lonesome One	

2. At the organ—SPIRITUALS

Among the spirituals Mr. Waller may play are the following:

> Go Down Moses
> Swing Low, Sweet Chariot
> Deep River
> All God's Chillun Got Wings
> Water Boy
> Sometimes I Feel Like a Motherless Child
> Lonesome Road

At the organ—A MELODY

This selection, says Mr. Waller, was inspired by 8 bars of Sir Edward Elgar's Pomp and Circumstance.

3. At the piano—IMPROVISATIONS

Mr. Waller may be expected to begin this part of the program by playing:
> The Blues, in A

He will then improvise on some of the songs which he has recorded. For example:
> I'm Gonna Sit Right Down And
> Write Myself A Letter

He will then play:
> The Blues, in B flat

In this last improvisation Mr. Waller will be accompanied by Hot Lips Page, cornetist, who will sing and play his own blues.

— INTERMISSION —

4. At the piano—LONDON SUITE, 1939

This six part piano suite is an impressionistic sketch of pre-war London. Written in 1939 during Mr. Waller's last European tour, he first played it at the Salle Pleyel in Paris, and later recorded it as an album in London. The album has never been released in this country.

1. Soho	4. Whitechapel
2. Mayfair	5. Limehouse
3. Bond Street	6. Piccadilly Circus

At the piano—VARIATIONS ON A TCHAIKOVSKY THEME

5. At the organ—GERSHWINIANA

Musicologists often refer to the broad influence of the blues on the works of George Gershwin. This group of variations on Gershwin popular themes will provide illustration for this point. Among the Gershwin songs that may be played are:

> Bidin' My Time
> But Not For Me
> Embraceable You
> Feeling I'm Falling
> How Long Has This Been Going On
> I've Got A Crush On You
> Liza
> Luckiest Man In the World
> Man I Love
> My One and Only
> Oh Lady Be Good
> Sam and Delilah
> Somebody Loves Me
> Someone To Watch Over Me
> Strike Up The Band
> Summertime
> Swanee
> Sweet and Low Down
> Who Cares
> Why Do I Love You

At the piano—VARIATIONS ON A THEME BY GEORGE GERSHWIN

Assisted by Mr. Bud Freeman, Mr. Waller plays a composition inspired by Gershwin's I Got Rhythm.

6. Orchestral group—FATS WALLER AND THE CHICAGOANS. *Assisting Artists are*: Eddie Condon, Guitar; John Kirby, Bass; Gene Krupa, Drums; Bud Freeman, Tenor Saxophone; Pee Wee Russell, Clarinet; Max Kaminsky, Cornet.

Mr. Waller will play a group of impromptu selections with the leaders of the Chicago style.
Among the tunes these musicians may play are:
> China Boy
> I Found a New Baby
> Honeysuckle Rose
> "Havin' a Ball at Carnegie Hall,"
> an improvised fast blues.

Steinway Piano — Hammond Organ — Victor Records

Mr. Waller is presented in this recital by
ERNEST ANDERSON

485 Madison Avenue   New York City

b. Sidney Bechet

one indulgence from the audience," said the program. "Most of the people on the program are making their first appearance before a predominantly white audience; many of them have never visited the North before. They will do their very best if the audience will cooperate with them by creating an atmosphere of informality and interest. The most memorable hot music comes when the performer can feel his audience. May we ask that you forget you are in Carnegie Hall?" William "Big Bill" Broonzy, Chicago farmhand by day and Vocalion recording star by night, met his first white audience at this concert. Meade "Lux" Lewis, king of the railroad-piano blues, quit his job as a Chicago handyman to make this concert date.

That year, 1938, was the last year of peace in the Western world, but already the old

c. Sister Rosetta Tharpe

a. Pete Johnson

b. "Sonny" Terry

c. Albert Ammons, Meade "Lux" Lewis

standards were falling away and new forces were at work in the body politic and the body social. Nine years of the Great Depression, five years of the New Deal, upheaval, change—these had comprised the daily diet of many Americans. Proletarian literature, the new realism, had made its impression; but the probing went deeper: Richard Wright's *Uncle Tom's Children* was published, MacLeish's *Land of the Free,* Sherwood's *Abe Lincoln in Illinois,* and John Dewey's *Experience and Education* appeared—contributions toward a firmer definition of America's egalitarian democracy. Among the deeper meanings was this: the color line had to go. For jazz in 1938, this was important. "From Spirituals to Swing" was an all-Negro program; only the MC, John Hammond, was white: this marked the end of an era in music. But at the beginning of the year (January 16) a tuxedoed clarinetist named Benjamin David "Benny" Goodman walked onto the Carnegie stage with his full band, plus the famous quartet of Gene Krupa (drums), Teddy Wilson (piano), and Lionel Hampton (vibraphone) which had been knocking down color bars in clubs and theaters since 1935.

Although Goodman, at thirty, had already acquired a national reputation via his "Let's Dance" show on NBC-Radio and his many recordings, he was as nervous as a bridegroom before the big concert. He had done a little "papering" among friends to ensure a claque and had even asked comedienne Beatrice Lillie to join the program (she wisely declined).

Outside, the 16th was a bitter, cold evening; but inside the old Hall, where every seat was taken and several dozen more were crowded onstage, the evening was red hot. Goodman ran through much of his Henderson-Mundy-Sampson repertoire ("King Porter Stomp," "Copenhagen," "Stompin' at the Savoy"), but the highlight of this famous concert was the jam session (on Fats Waller's "Honeysuckle Rose") that involved, as Benny's guest stars, Johnny Hodges, Harry Carney, and Count Basie, plus Basie sidemen Freddie Green, Buck Clayton, Walter Page, and Lester Young. Bobby Hackett and Cootie Williams were also on hand. The rather stuffy plea of the "From Spirituals to Swing" program was not at all necessary for this one; the Carnegie crowd cheered every soloist and went wild over Jess Stacey's five slashing choruses of

a. Jimmy Rushing, Count Basie

b. Benny Goodman on stage stairs

"Sing, Sing, Sing." It was all wide-open music.

The era of the big band lasted till the end of the war and then went into a brief eclipse. For a short time the clock was turned back and the small, hot, two-beat combo was in furious demand. From out of the past came a host of new-old faces: Bunk Johnson, Kid Ory, Sidney Bechet, Art Hodes, Frankie Newton, Henry "Red" Allen. They took over the college dates and junior proms, the conventions, the theater gigs. They stimulated a mushrooming of jazz cellars and rathskellers and they traveled the roads in station wagons. Most of them had to be introduced to America all over again. But some, like Louis Armstrong, had always been there with stabbing improvisations.

One of King Louis's best nights was November 29, 1947, at the height of the Dixieland revival. He came into Carnegie Hall with his new sextet. For the previous decade or so Armstrong had been fronting a host of pickup big bands, taking an occasional chorus on his trumpet, but concentrating largely on his ability to mug out a lyric. But instead of wheeling in another large, anonymous band—obtained alphabetically from the AF of M roster—Louis

a. Hampton, Krupa, Wilson, Goodman

b. Goodman and band on stage

148

a. Louis Armstrong

b. Notice in Goodman's 1936 program

c. Will Bradley, Henry Levine, Bunny Berrigan, Charlie Shavers, Buck Clayton, Max Kaminsky

149

Duke Ellington

hand-picked a fine small group: Jack Teagarden (trombone), Barney Bigard (clarinet), Dick Cary (piano), Big Sid Catlett (drums), and Arvell Shaw (bass). The group was an immediate success.

Other Dixieland giants have had their day —or evening—in Carnegie Hall. A "Dixieland Holiday" of 1956 brought Max Kaminsky and his band together with Tony Parenti and his Rag Pickers (Milt Hinton, Dick Wellstood, and Tony Spargo), ending the show with Stan Rubin's Tiger Town Five. Rubin's appearance was one of many Ivy League ventures into jazz. A midnight show of 1957, titled "College

Goes to Jazz" (MC: Eddie Condon), featured Eli's Chosen Six, the Smithereens, the Six-Pence (University of Pennsylvania), the Brunotes (Brown), and six other jivey leaguers. Dixieland had its heyday in Carnegie Hall, but today it's unlikely that two-beat can draw a full house. Only another radical development in jazz (after bop—what?) will drive enough buffs back to the Rampart.

Goodman and Armstrong were two of the three great forces of pre-World War II jazz. The third was Edward Kennedy "Duke" Ellington. In 1922, on a tip from Fats Waller, Duke came north and joined his Washington,

a. Count Basie, Sarah Vaughan, Lester Young in Green Room

b. Eddie Condon

151

a. Charlie Parker and friend

D.C., friends (Otto Hardwick, Art Whetsol, Sonny Greer, and Elmer Snowden) in New York for a job in Barron's, one of the top Harlem clubs. Twenty music-filled years passed; then, in 1943, New Yorkers declared an "Ellington Week," highlighted by a big Ellington concert in Carnegie Hall. All seats were taken. Such highly respected critics as Briggs of the *Post*, Henry Simon of *PM*, and the *Sun's* Irving Kolodin (who also wrote the program notes) attended. Many of Duke's close friends were also there: Count Basie and Marian Anderson joined Eric Bernay; in a nearby box were John Hammond, the Benny Goodmans (with Sergeant Harry on leave), Moe Gale (Gale Music), and Duke's brother-in-law Dan James (Tempo Music); Jimmie Lunceford shared Jack Mills's (Mills Music) box; Jack Robbins (Robbins Music) and Ed Morris (Morris Music) were also there. Duke had become big business as well as big music.

Duke had been working on an opera *(Boola)* for years with little success. For this concert he sifted through *Boola*, added new material, and came up with a "Tone Parallel to the History of the Negro in America." He called the forty-five-minute work *Black, Brown, and Beige*. Although *BBB* pushed up through new ground, its roots were firm in jazz antecedents. But most critics were either lukewarm or unim-

b. Dizzy Gillespie

b. Dave Brubeck

pressed. (Said the *Tribune*'s Paul Bowles: "Nothing emerged but a gaudy potpourri of tutti dance passages and solo virtuoso work.") For musicians and jazzophiles, however, Duke was once again leading the profession forward. He returned twice more to Carnegie Hall that year, ending in December with the premiere of a concerto based on Roi Ottley's book, *New World A-Coming.* Other Carnegie premieres followed: *Liberian Suite, The Tattooed Bride, Blue Bell of Harlem,* and (with the Symphony of the Air) *Night Creature* in 1955.

Duke has had a number of fine vocalists with his band—Lena Horne, Ivie Anderson, Joya Sherrill, Kay Davis—but one singer was missing: Billie Holiday.

Billie appeared at Carnegie several times, but her program of November 10, 1956, was something special. She hadn't sung in New York for three years; the city had taken away her cabaret card, prohibiting her from working where liquor was sold. This denial of work was another in a series of defeats for Billie—some of them asked for, some unfairly delivered. In 1956, following the successful publication of her autobiography, her friends staged a Carnegie program for her, using the title of

a. Miles Davis

b. Illinois Jacquet

c. Oscar Peterson

e. Gerry Mulligan

d. Stan Getz (holding tenor sax) and Coleman Hawkins

a. Benny Goodman with Philharmonic under Barbirolli

b. Joseph Szigeti and Benny Goodman

her book, *Lady Sings the Blues. Times* writer Gilbert Millstein narrated parts of the book and Billie sang the music that best expressed her troubled life. Behind, on a darkened stage, were Coleman Hawkins, Buck Clayton, Roy Eldridge, Al Cohn, Kenny Burrell, and Carl Drinkered. It was, in the opinion of her admirers, her greatest performance, her last great stand. Billie had once said, "If you find a tune, and it's got something to do with you, you don't have to work at it. You just feel it, and when you feel it, other people feel something, too." That November evening, a packed house felt the greatness of Billie Holiday, a unique figure in jazz.

Billie's concert was a high point in jazz history, but it was not the only important postwar jazz concert in Carnegie Hall. On September 29, 1947, the dynamic leader of the new "bop" movement, John Birks "Dizzy" Gillespie, gave his first concert in the Hall. He had two featured soloists: Ella Fitzgerald and Charlie "Bird" Parker. The band was a big one; in fact, it was the first full bop band to be formed. Among its personnel were many graduates of Minton's and The Street (Fifty-second), just five blocks south of Carnegie. The new phrasings, the new range of harmonies, and the new pacings worked out in small tight groups on the bandstand of The Three Deuces were now presented in formal concert. Pianist John Lewis offered his *Toccata for Solo Trumpet and Orchestra,* and George Russell had his "Cubana-Be" and "Cubana-Bop" performed (with the great Chano Pozo, from Matanzas, Cuba, on the bongo drums). Russell's Afro-Cuban bop breakthrough at this concert gave "hard-bop" devotees something to study and emulate for years to come.

The appearance of Charlie Parker on this

Woody, Stravinsky and The Herd rehearsing "Ebony Concerto"

Stan Kenton and his orchestra

date rounded out the picture of jazz leadership. Gillespie and Parker were both virtuosos on their instruments, splendid in technique and innovation. "Bird," in particular, drove forward with reckless excitement. Listeners were more breathless listening to "Ko-Ko," "Red Cross," and "How High the Moon" than was the round-faced, round-figured man blowing the sounds on alto.

The history of jazz tends to polarize around a few men: Jim Europe, W. C. Handy, Benny Goodman, Parker and Gillespie, Armstrong and Ellington. They were all musicians. But a man of equal importance to jazz and to the history of Carnegie Hall plays no instrument and has only a passing knowledge of written music. Norman Granz put together his first big jazz show in 1946 at the Los Angeles Philharmonic Hall. It was a sellout. Granz took his Jazz at the Philharmonic across the country, creating sensations in Symphony Hall (Boston), the Academy of Music (Philadelphia), and Carnegie Hall. Purists denounced Granz's Barnum approach, but the net effect

Maynard Ferguson soloing with his orchestra

was impressive. Serving in his jazz battalions were Stan Getz, Oscar Peterson, Flip Philips, Howard McGhee, Lester Young, Ella Fitzgerald, and many more. Out of the tent-show "battles of music" came an audience for the Young Turks of cool jazz, including Getz, Gerry Mulligan, Lennie Tristano, John Lewis, and Miles Davis.

In 1955 Dave Brubeck came out of the west to make the cover of *Time*. The Friedman and Gardiner office brought the Brubeck Quartet to Carnegie on a program shared by Mulligan, Chet Baker, and vocalist Carmen McRae. It was a program of buttoned-down jazz: Brubeck's scholarly improvisations and Mulligan's austere pianoless harmonies. The Mulligan and Brubeck groups were in top form that night, March 12, 1955. However, newspapers the next day reported instead the untimely

death of Charles "Bird" Parker, the man who made the previous night's music possible.

The small combo is still a staple of jazz. Carnegie has played host to many, including John Lewis's Modern Jazz Quartet, the pickup groups of Thelonius Monk, the Sonny Rollins Trio, the Phineas Newborn Quartet, and many others. But the big-band era is far from over. A key personality here is Woodrow Charles "Woody" Herman. Woody organized his first "Herd" in 1943, featuring Chubby Jackson, Neal Hefti, Flip Philips, Bill Harris, Pete Candoli, and Sonny Berman. This is the herd he brought to Carnegie in March, 1946, in a milestone concert. Among the highlights: Ralph Burns's four-part *Summer Sequence* and a special score by Igor Stravinsky, *Ebony Concerto*. (Stravinsky was to have conducted it at the Hall; however, illness prevented him

Composer Teo Macero (left center, in front of mellophone) in rehearsal

Composer Gunther Schuller reviews score with bassists in studio

from doing so at the last moment.) Woody's 1946 program represents the culmination of many years' development, from the 1924 Gershwin-Whiteman concert and the 1943 Ellington efforts, toward a marriage of jazz with classical music. Woody and Stravinsky tied the knot in Carnegie Hall. Since then music schools (Juilliard, Curtis Institute, Tanglewood), foundations, and conductors (Bernstein, Mitropoulos, Stokowski) have advanced the cause. New composers have appeared from the ranks of jazz: Teddy Charles, Mal Waldron, Gunther Schuller, and Teo Macero (a leading figure in the Jazz Composers Workshop). Their serious works have not only been introduced

in Carnegie Recital Hall, but in the main hall as well. One of the most significant jazz-symphonic programs was given in 1960 by the Orchestra of America under Richard Korn. It featured Benny Goodman in Copland's *Concerto for Clarinet*, the Modern Jazz Quartet in Schuller's *Concertino for Jazz Quartet and Orchestra*, Kreutz's *Dixieland Concerto*, and Antheil's *Jazz Symphony*. Clearly, there was enough in the serious jazz literature to sustain a program of high interest.

Jazz was first heard in the main hall when the Clef Club played it in 1912. A half-century later jazz is still being heard in the same hall and played by symphony orchestras.

161

Charles Dana Gibson in his studio

9 * The Upper Floors

THE main hall is like our living room. It's a showplace where we can demonstrate to the public the best things we can do. But back here in the studios is where the real work of our home goes on. It's like any other good home. You prepare for your company by sprucing up, trying out new recipes or cocktails, changing things around a little. Then, when your company arrives, you all go into the living room for the results. That's the way we feel about living and working in Carnegie Hall.

These sentiments by tenant Phil Moore, pianist-arranger-composer, lie at the core of what living in a Carnegie studio means. Because all its tenants are either in the arts or dabble in occult movements, Carnegie has been nicknamed "Upper Bohemia." But it is quite unlike "Lower Bohemia" (Greenwich Village). Although not high for its neighborhood, Carnegie quarters are still expensive: two rooms for $250 a month is not unusual. It must be remembered that the nature of the building requires constant watching by uniformed attendants; one of the comforting things about living in Carnegie Hall is the knowledge that the elevator staff will brook no nonsense from strangers with no excuse for entering. Also, a trash and garbage collection staff is necessary, since incinerator chutes—common enough in buildings built for residence—were not in the original plans. (One of Simon, Jr.'s, harassment techniques for expelling tenants in 1959–1960 was to curtail garbage collections, according to the irate residents who stuck it

out.) These and other services peculiar to this building add to the costs of living there.

To meet the rent and the other expenses of being in the arts (clothes, music, accompanists, canvas, scripts, tutoring, etc.) the Carnegie tenant is an exceptionally hard-working, hard-driving individual. Dilettantes and beatniks are hopelessly outclassed: Carnegie is the home of the true professional. While Greenwich Village is famous for an "open-door" atmosphere—neighbors informally drifting in and out of each other's "pads"—Carnegie is known for having very little idle socializing among its tenants: everyone is busy working, planning, hoping.

Another difference between the Carnegie Hall environment and any other artists' haven is the fact that the finest musical performances to be heard anywhere in the world are being shaped, rehearsed, and performed in the several halls. "When I was tired of an afternoon or evening, I used to slip into the [main] auditorium, listen to all or part of a symphony, and derive rest and inspiration," wrote Edwin Howland Blashfield, muralist who occupied Studio 823 for over thirty-five years. It is this proximity to—and intimacy with—big events, drawing big audiences, which makes a Carnegie home so desirable.

In the early days of the Hall the spaces in the upper floors were designed for lodge meetings or business offices. The addition of skylights and duplex windows brought in a host of artists who are characteristically heliotropic.

But few tenants lived there. Charles Dana Gibson, turning out Gibson girls by the score, worked in Studio 90 for thirty-three years, but maintained a town house in the East Seventies. Among his contemporaries, some like-minded about the separation of home and studio, were George Inness, Jr. (landscape and animal painter and son of the famous George Inness, landscape painter), Frederick S. Church (illustrator of *Alice in Wonderland*, kept a small menagerie in his studio for animal-painting models), impressionist Childe Hassam (landscapes and some interiors), and several more descendants of the literalist Hudson River School. Most recently, *New Yorker* illustrator Victor Pauw, Zoltan Hecht, Robert Philipp, Gustav Rehberger, and Sidney Dickinson have been painting and Ian McLeod has been sculpting there. (Paul Swan is still painting and sculpting, but he's also dancing and writing.) These later artists count Carnegie as their permanent residence.

Music teachers began infiltrating the Hall early, because its thick masonry walls offered soundproof studios. Here William Thorner taught voice to Rosa Ponselle, Galli-Curci, and Al Jolson. Mme. Annette Wolter, Walter O. Robinson, and "Duchess" Ethel Edwards taught voice and elocution here, also.

In Studio 905, a tiny corner space, Mrs. Lucy A. Alexander has been teaching piano for thirty-two years. Mrs. Alexander was a friend of pianist-composer-teacher Edward MacDowell. The MacDowell Club—later the MacDowell

Mrs. Lucy Alexander's Studio 905, southeastern exposure (Fifty-sixth Street)

Association—was formed in neighbor Eugene Heffley's studio. There used to be a gigantic bathtub occupying a good third of the space (an eccentricity of a former tenant) until the thirties, when Mrs. Alexander installed a shower and cooking facilities.

The acoustical brilliance of the several Carnegie auditoriums is present in many of the studios, too. Enrico Caruso was taken up to Studio 826 by the Victor Talking Machine Company to make his first recording. Small radio stations, such as the now-defunct foreign language WFAB, used to broadcast from Carnegie studios. (WOR broadcast radio programs from Carnegie first in 1927. Before long such shows as *The Telephone Hour, Jessel's Variety Hour, Ward Family Theater*, and *Stoopnagle and Bud* originated from the Carnegie pre-

a. Caruso (right) hears playback of record made in Studio 826 (below)

b. Fashion photographer Ray Solowinski has Studio 826, western exposure (Seventh Avenue)

Mlle. Beauvais at the piano in Studio 868-869, southern exposure

cincts.) Engineers recall glowingly the old Carnegie Recording Studio, a cramped room made even more cramped by a concert grand piano. In the days before wire or magnetic tape, such artists as Kenneth Spencer, Vladimir Horowitz, and Pete Seeger sang or played into a big, wire-hung microphone and watched the stylus carve out a master in a corner of the room.

Although most studios have full, high ceilings, those on "8 Mezz" are only seven feet high. It is an intervening, or mezzanine, floor that has always puzzled the purists. However, Mlle. Jeanne Beauvais, living in 868-9, is happy and unconcerned. She has lived there for nearly eighteen years (arriving as a teen-ager, it should be noted). Whether at home or on tour, Mlle. Beauvais keeps her studio crowded with fellow performers: Jan Peerce, Eileen Farrell, Cesare Siepi, Jenny Tourel, the Bach Aria group, and the "After-Dinner Opera Company," a trio of singers which includes Mlle. Beauvais. They all rehearse in her studio and eat hasty meals in her kitchen. She herself has sung in the main hall, on television, and most recently scored a triumph in the roles of "Mme. DuBonnet" and "Polly" in the off-Broadway musical hit *The Boy Friend.*

Pietro Yon was one of the finest organists New York has ever heard. He played the giant instrument at St. Patrick's Cathedral for twenty-seven years. It was a Kilgren, as was

a. Pietro Yon

the fourteen-stop instrument built into his sixth-floor studio. Fortunately the thunder of his studio organ was muffled by the three-foot-thick masonry walls of his apartment. Yon also played the five-ton Carnegie organ with the Philharmonic and with visiting orchestras.

Yon's prize pupil was Miss Emilia Del Terzo. She was not quite sixteen when she rented her own tiny studio in the building; Miss Leonora Shier, Carnegie's former "housemother," was assigned as Emilia's guardian. Miss Del Terzo not only developed into a fine organist, but could cook, too. Not infrequently, Pietro Yon and his good friend Arturo Toscanini would escape to Miss Del Terzo's for a complete and authentic Italian dinner and hours of animated talk. When Yon passed away, Miss Del Terzo was offered his delightful studio overlooking Fifty-seventh Street. She made a low-ceilinged

b. Miss Del Terzo at the organ in Studio 851-2-3 (real pipes are behind false pipes on the left)

a. Claudia Lyon and New School recorder class in second room of three-room Del Terzo suite

b. Same room, other end, northern exposure (Fifty-seventh Street)

duplex apartment out of one half; the other, still housing the huge Kilgren, retains the high ceiling and the comfort of an old shoe.

There are approximately 170 studios in Carnegie Hall—"approximately" because the tenants absorb neighboring studios in good times and divide up studios in bad times. Artists, being staunch individualists, must rearrange apartments to suit their own needs—and frequently do. The studios of Marc Connelly and Paddy Chayefsky differed from each other as both did from the studios of John Barrymore and Marlon Brando. But the building itself, unlike many modern buildings, has the strong basic structure to allow for any eccentricities.

For seven decades Carnegie Hall has been the home of busy invention. And from this pleasant hive have come the honey and flame of much of our cultural history.

John Jacob Niles

10 * Ballads and
Folk Songs

A LEAN, long-jawed ridge runner named John Jacob Niles appeared in Carnegie Hall the week before Christmas, 1932, and strummed and sang a program of holiday and folk music. Although many vocalists before him had included a folk song or two in their programs, the Niles appearance was the first true folk music event in the main hall. And 1932 was, after all, a perfect year to celebrate the music of the common people on the world's greatest stage. The Chicago and Philadelphia Opera Houses gave no performances that year; there were thirteen million unemployed (a thousand of them formed the "Bonus Army" march on Washington); the big Tin Pan Alley hit was "Brother, Can You Spare a Dime?"; *Tobacco Road* was published; and scientists probed into the "principle of uncertainty."

During the thirties, proletarian writers, artists, and singers pursued the homely American with unflagging ardor. The paths frequently wound in and out of Carnegie studios, where singers gave informal performances or, like Niles, popped up on unscheduled, unadvertised programs. During World War II Josh White sang folk blues on a Count Basie program at Carnegie, and few "monster" War Bond rallies were considered "balanced" or "representative" without at least one folk singer on hand. The first big postwar folk concert was produced by Alan Lomax on April 29, 1946. "Folk Song Jamboree" featured Huddie "Leadbelly" Ledbetter, Woody Guthrie, Josh White, Carl Sandburg, Richard Dyer-Bennett, Lee Hays, and the Hall Johnson choir.

Intelligently conceived and advertised, "Folk Song Jamboree" was a huge success and did much to stimulate—at least in New York—the folk renaissance of the fifties. The next concert of note was the first of many hootenannies at Carnegie Hall. It was produced in December, 1947, by People's Songs, a loose confederation of folk singers, students, and trade unionists. This was also the first midnight concert ever held at Carnegie. Pete Seeger flew in from California to headline the all-star show. Then, in 1949, E. Y. Harburg staged "A Musical Tapestry," with script by Norman Corwin. Behind the drawn gray stage curtain nearly two dozen folk singers with guitars and banjos were joined by technicians, plus Artie Shaw and his string orchestra. They all became embroiled, says the program's MC Oscar Brand, in "probably the worst traffic jam in the history of the Hall!"

The acknowledged mistress of gospel singing, Miss Mahalia Jackson, gave the first of her annual Carnegie recitals in 1950. Born in the dockside slums of New Orleans, schooled in Chicago's Bronzeville ghetto, Miss Jackson found relief and meaning in life in the gospel music of her church. Her power is now legend, her scoops and slides imitated but rarely achieved by others.

Recently the dominant folk event has been the hootenanny. (One alleged root of this word is "hootin' Annie.") These programs have enjoyed some of the liveliest, largest audiences in the history of the Hall, with standees against every wall as a matter of course. (Pete Seeger's

a. Woody Guthrie

b. Richard Dyer-Bennett

Mahalia Jackson

rousing audience of 2,900-plus in September, 1959, is one unforgettable example.) The first hoots were staged as Sunday afternoon rent parties by the Almanac Singers, with Woody, Josh, Burl Ives, and Millard Lampell among the voices raised. They were put on in such modest auditoriums as Newspaper Guild Hall, Manhattan Center (when the "over-28" clubs weren't dancing there), and the ballroom of District 65 of the Wholesale and Ware-housemen's Union. Finally the big jump was made to Carnegie Hall. People's Songs, later *Sing Out!* magazine, produced them. The Carnegie hoots had a lively young lady as stage manager until her play opened on Broadway: Lorraine Hansberry of *A Raisin in the Sun*.

The development of the folk idiom has taken some curious turns. In the thirties and forties, singers picked up songs as they found them and asked no questions. During the fif-

Harry Belafonte

a. Theodore Bikel

b. Oscar Brand

c. Josh White

ties, however, the fashion was to search for a scholarly context for each song. (John Greenway, the singing professor, is fond of Walt Whitman's lines: "No one will ever get at my verses who insists upon viewing them as a literary performance. . . .") Oddly enough the first to produce an intellectually conceived program of folk music was Alan Lomax, the young genius behind the 1946 "Folk Song Jamboree." In 1949 Lomax became fascinated with rock 'n' roll, rockabilly, the "big beat," and the new look on the old "race record" catalogues. He immersed himself in total listening, then rose to the surface with a historical overview of folk and popular music: "Folk Song '59," a rambling web of work songs, street gospel, backwater blues, cowboy balladeering, hillbilly hoke, and rock 'n' roll.

Ed McCurdy

Memphis Slim, Muddy Waters, Jimmy Driftwood, and others showed up. (But the advertised star of this outré program, rock 'n' roller Bobby Darin, failed to appear.) Except for this puzzling interlude, the folk programs of Carnegie Hall have been frankly presented without explanation or apology.

Honest, authentic programs have been given by many excellent artists. Harry Belafonte first appeared in a one-man show (1953) that packed the Hall. In April, 1959, he appeared two evenings in a row as benefits for the New Lincoln and the Wiltwyck Schools. Belafonte has also introduced Odetta and Miriam Makeba on his programs. Theodore Bikel made his New York debut (1956) in a concert of international folk music in Recital Hall. Also in and out of Recital Hall has been a parade of such banjo virtuosos as Bob Gibson, Billy Faier, and Erik Darling in programs produced by Israel Young, knowledgeable heritor of the Folk Music Center, Greenwich Village. Carnegie has also been host to other "second-generation" folk singers like the New Lost City Ramblers (Mike Seeger, Tom Paley, John Cohen), Leon Bibb, Will Holt, Frank Hamilton, Guy Carawan, Elly Stone (on a program with satirist Tom Lehrer), and the Tarriers. Among the youngest to appear were the ten- and eleven-year-old boys of the Wiltwyck School Steel Band, under their Trinidadian director, Kim Loy Fong. With ten steel drums, a cowbell, and a pair of maracas they delighted a packed house with muffled thunder and free-form harmonics. "They received an uproarious ovation from the audience," *Times* critic John S. Wilson reported, "which was so taken with the band's playing that every selection was broken into by billows of applause."

As with jazz, the early folk music of America measured the contours and challenges of this continent. But, as recent Carnegie programs indicate, today's singers are reaching into Asia, Africa, and the Middle East for new material. Few now spend their hours onstage without offering an Indonesian lullaby, an Angolan spiritual, or an Israeli shepherd's song. The recent commercial success of folk music is not the next logical development of the art in this country, as Lomax temporarily thought. Its true development has been to follow America's own expanding horizons west to the Mississippi and the Pacific and south to the Caribbean, eventually bridging the oceans to other continents.

With the nationhood of many African states, more attention has been given to that continent's special contributions. Folk singers Robert Le House (Sudan) and Miriam Makeba (South Africa) have been warmly received in their Carnegie débuts. Nigeria has had a special place of importance. (On the classical side,

The Weavers, from left: Erik Darling, Ronnie Gilbert, Fred Hellerman and Lee Hays

Burl Ives

a. Ronnie Gilbert in Green Room for intermission

b. Odetta on stage

Fela Sowande, conducting 85 members of the Philharmonic, introduced his *Folk Symphony* to America in Carnegie Hall, June, 1962, a work commissioned by the Nigerian government in honor of their 1960 independence.) Among the most interesting Nigerian visitors in the folk field has been Babatunde Olatunji.

In a midnight concert in April, 1962, Olatunji presented his "Drums of Passion" company in a program of rain-forest rhythms. (This was not his first appearance in the Hall, however; two years before, while enrolled at Morehouse College, Atlanta, Olatunji played drums in a giant international folk program produced by

Odetta and bass accompanist Larry tuning up in Green Room

Babatunde Olatunji

the Slavinsky family and their century-old Russian chorus.)

Forty years ago Huddie Ledbetter stayed close to his land; today, one of Leadbelly's heirs, Pete Seeger, travels beyond it, picking out the dreams and aspirations of *all* lands on the humble banjo and guitar. He sang it in a post-Christmas 1957 concert:

Passing through, passing through,
Sometimes happy, sometimes blue,
Glad that I ran into you.
Tell the people that you saw me
Passing through . . .

His pathways for that concert lay in three continents.

Isadora Duncan with the "Isadorables"

11 * Dance

IN ALL four of its stages and in a score of its studios, Carnegie Hall has contributed much to the history of dance in America. Before 1911 Carnegie programs generally reflected popular American tastes. Minstrel shows, such as *Fun on the Levee,* were all the rage, running second only to the dazzling Broadway spectaculars. The turning point came in 1910, when the Imperial Russian Ballet and Orchestra arrived at the Metropolitan, featuring Anna Pavlova (*prima ballerina assoluta*) and Mikhail Mordkin (*premier danseur classique*). This company, in New York and on tour, woke America to the art and beauty of a ballet program. Interest in serious dance was effectively kindled. However, the Pavlova-Mordkin tour had hardly begun when Isadora Duncan (whose family had lived briefly in a Carnegie studio) returned from Europe and gave a Carnegie recital of her "free form" dancing. Her 1911 audience was not completely ready for it; the informal costuming, the highly individual interpretations, the solo dancing to the symphonies of Beethoven, Wagner, and Schubert (Walter Damrosch conducting the Philharmonic) were beyond the ken of her audiences.

Isadora returned to Europe, settling finally in Lenin's Russia and visiting the United States infrequently. Her last appearance here in 1922 began with *opera buffa* at Ellis Island (she had married Russian pseudo-poet Serge Essenine, whose passport was not in order) and ended with a *coup de theâtre* in Carnegie Hall.

"America has all that Russia has not! Why will not America reach out its hand to Russia, as I have given my hand?" she cried to a startled audience. Isadora's "children," top students from her Russian school, accompanied her. Popularly called "The Isadorables," they returned to Carnegie after the bizarre death of their great teacher in 1927. The Duncan name is still very much with us, however; brother Raymond Duncan is every bit as free a spirit as was his famous sister: he still prefers a loose toga to more conventional dress and makes excellent thong sandals by hand. His participation in the dance is probably more spectacular. A typical Raymond Duncan program took place, for example, in the spring of 1962. It was a "spontaneous creation" called "GREEN LIGHTS, a three-act fantasy in Colour." The program notes, which always have the ring of a manifesto, explained that "Humanity takes refuge in the rainbow. There is Open Choice."

Ruth St. Denis, the "Jersey Hindoo," also sought liberation through the dance; shocked everybody with her sensuous "Radha"; and championed Orientalism in American ballet. She and Isadora came to ballet through a stage door: Ruth as protégée of David Belasco, Isadora as chorus girl for Augustin Daly. "I was born into a world of splits and kicks in vaudeville," Miss St. Denis has written, "and a completely moribund ballet at the opera." Among the most frequent dance recitalists at Carnegie Hall were Ruth St. Denis, her husband Ted

Ted Shawn and Ruth St. Denis

Shawn, and their company of Denishawn Dancers. However, the real story of Carnegie balletics is up in the studios.

Among the most famous ballet studios in the world is Studio 61, Ballet Arts. This large studio-suite was originally a boys' gymnasium; later, occult psychology was taught in it; for a while John Bovington used it as his Church of the Dance ("Let us now draw love in the air," etc.); and in 1937 some members of the Abraham Lincoln Brigade taught Marxist history there while on furlough from the Spanish Civil War. But ballet has been the principal tenant since 1912, when Alys Bentley, in Grecian robes, taught the disciplines of the new ballet to such students as Sonia and Jerome

Yeichi Nimura in a spear dance

a. Lisan Kay instructing a class in Ballet Arts, Studio 61

b. Yeichi Nimura teaching a group

188

Robbins, Agnes de Mille, and Margaret D'Houbler. Miss Bentley offered 61 as a haven for Isadora and her Duncan-trained dancers; for Michio Ito, who brought authenticity and vitality to Orientalism; and eventually—but decidedly against her will—for those who, with the aid of showman John Murray Anderson, wished to study musical comedy, opera, and chorus line, too. Miss Bentley split with Virginia Lee, a dancer-turned-entrepreneur, on the future conduct of the school—and Miss Bentley lost. Virginia Lee, however, had a strong bargaining position, as the manager of Ito's remarkable Japanese discovery, Yeichi Nimura.

The Lee-Nimura superintendency of Studio 61 for the past two decades has been preeminent. With its two annexes, Ballet Arts is one of New York's largest studios (3,500 square feet), and has been close to ideal for planning and rehearsing such large productions as Michel Fokine's *Les Sylphides*, the Mordkin-Lucia Chase *Giselle*, Gian-Carlo Menotti's *Sebastian*, CBS-TV's "Gold Rush" ballet for *Seven Lively Arts*, and Agnes de Mille's flamboyant *Rodeo*. Isadora, Denishawn, and Louis Horst and Martha Graham (who also occupied a seventh-floor studio) worked out many new dances here. When Roland Petit's, Sadler's Wells, or any other touring company arrives in New York, their dancers individually or as a corps naturally gravitate to Ballet Arts for lessons and practice. An average day's classes may include hours in toe, supported adagio, jazz, modern Oriental, and kathak Hindu. Teaching these are such dance stars as Lisan

Group from "Lute Song" includes Raymond Scott (fourth from left), Mary Martin (seated center), Clarence Derwent (standing, behind Miss Martin's chair), Nancy Davis and Lisan Kay (right, behind Miss Martin), Nimura (seated, right), Ron Fletcher (on floor, far right)

a. Agnes de Mille in a figure from "Rodeo"

b. Helen Wood

190

Kay, a European-acclaimed soloist; Henry Danton, soloist with International Ballet and Sadler's Wells; Vladimir Konstantinov, student of Agrippina Vaganova in old Petrograd; Nina Stroganova, student of Olga Preobrajenska and a guest ballerina with Ballet Russe de Monte Carlo; Vladimir Dokoudovsky, former partner of the great Preobrajenska, *premier danseur* for Nijinska's Polish Ballet and the Original Ballet Russe (and Nina Stroganova's husband), Yeichi Nimura, and Agnes De Mille, who is also a coproprietor of Ballet Arts. Among their students: skating champions Carol and Nancy Heiss, Yul Brynner, Julie Newmar, Radio City's dancer-singer-violinist Helen Wood, Patrice Munsel, Bambi Linn, and Mary Martin. Among its recent crop of young stars is tall (6′1″), handsome Dean Crane, veteran of television (*Phil Silvers Show, Ed Sullivan Show*), films (*Ben Hur, Naked Maja*), circuses (clown, aerialist, and daredevil equestrian), and an impressive ballet soloist for whom Nimura personally does the notation.

Before leaving Studio 61, a footnote about its pianists. Plodding through *Nutcracker* with careful metronomics is no mean trick, particularly when the previous hour was a jazz lesson and the following hour will be *Billy the Kid*. For the past fifteen years Charles Biddleman has ruled 61's well worn keyboard. Intermittent pianists have included Leonard Bernstein and composer John Childs, Jr. These accompanists form a special fraternity within ballet.

In Carnegie's other major studio, the International Dance Studio in 819, Fedor Lensky presides over a faculty that includes Vitale Fokine (son of the famed Russian innovator Michel Fokine), Frank Wagner (a leading choreographer of industrial and trade shows), and Harry Woolever (veteran of *My Fair Lady*). Lensky himself was a student of Victor Gsovsky and modernists Rudolph Laban and Kurt Jooss. He was ballet master and first soloist with the Nouveau Ballet de Monte Carlo, among other early assignments. He works six days a week from 11 A.M. to 9 P.M., normal ballet hours. Among Lensky's students have been France Nuyen, Dody Goodman, Chita Rivera, Gwen Verdon, and Monique

a. Vladimir Dokoudovsky and Nina Stroganova (Dokoudovsky)

b. Dean Crane and Asia

Van Vooren. Studio 819, with its clerestory and high, sloping skylight, is an ideal dance environment and was once rented by Mikhail Mordkin and Michel Fokine in the twenties.

Lensky tells how he came to operate a ballet studio in the first place. "I used to tour with my company—but after a while I couldn't take it. It's not like touring with a dog act. With the little dogs you have no trouble: you put them in a box and mail them to the next theater. But not so with the kids! One gets married, another gets sick, someone else is pregnant —it becomes too much. No, I'm very happy here in my studio." Is it difficult to get a good faculty together? "Not at all. In New York there are more teachers than students, so I can choose only those who will do the best by my students, who come here to work hard and learn."

It sounds elementary, but it isn't. In these two schools (Ballet Arts and International Dance Studio) and in the several other studios occupied by dancers and choreographers, the accent is on work; the sense of urgency is deeply felt. An average dancer, unlike a performer in other arts, is under a double handicap: the span of his peak dancing period will most likely be a decade or less (from sixteen to twenty-six, says Miss De Mille); and the human body, unless rigorously exercised every day throughout the year, tends to lose its tone. Ballet is also the only art form that has not

Fedor Lensky, director of the International Dance Studio (819)

M. Lensky drills his students at the barre

benefited by any twentieth-century technology; except for an occasional film or videotape, the performance survives only in the memory of the performer: he must physically repeat it. Despite an appalling ignorance and lack of interest by Americans, native choreographers and dancers have become the equal, and often the masters, of French, Russian, and British companies. And one could say that this superb native genius could count among its few homes Mr. Carnegie's fine old Hall.

Early in the Hall's history, 1896 to be precise, the already mentioned *Fun on the Levee* was performed by a group of amateurs. It was typical dance fare for a country that either square danced in barns and carriage houses or followed the *haute couture* ballroom rules of Dodworth's Dancing Academy. Frontier the-aters specialized in cancan, and Broadway choruses put the accent on beauty and costuming. Except for the grand tour of Fanny Elssler in 1840–1842, when President Martin Van Buren and his Cabinet received her and Congress adjourned to attend her performances, ballet was a minor entertainment. Original American works—excluding tiresome panto-mimes and shuffling minstrelsy—did not appear until George Washington Smith, whom dance historians call "the nation's first genuine *premier danseur*," choreographed the six-hour dance epic *The Black Crook* in 1866. This piece is indestructible; nearly everyone, including Agnes de Mille, has updated it. Things took a turn for the better, though, when Pavlova and Mordkin danced *Coppelia* at the Opera House on February 28, 1910.

a. La Argentina

b. Carmen Amaya

Farther up Seventh Avenue, Carnegie Hall also passed from cancan to capriole.

In addition to Isadora Duncan's recitals in Carnegie Hall, the Adolph Bolm Ballet Intime appeared in 1920. Denishawn exotica followed. La Argentina (Antonia Mercé) took Carnegie and all New York by storm in 1928. (Her matinee recital at the Maxine Elliott Theatre twelve years before had been snubbed by everyone.) Probably the most outstanding Spanish dancer of them all, La Argentina gave as many as thirty-eight performances a season —and all were sold out.

La Argentina is not to be confused with Argentinita (Encarnación López), who excited Carnegie audiences in a 1943 program shared by her sister Pilar López and José Greco. (Nor should her sister be confused with Pilar Gómez and her Mexico City dance company which made its Carnegie début in 1962!) Since her 1942 program, flamenco dancer Carmen Amaya (and family) has appeared, as well as Antonio and Rosario ("The Kids from Seville") and Roberto Iglesias, a dynamic young flamenco dancer who made his début at Carnegie in 1957. Still with us, after forty brilliant years, is Vincente Escudero, once La Argentina's partner.

For about a year (1956 especially) the calypso rage swept the country, but its New York headquarters was unquestionably Carnegie Recital Hall, where nearly every weekend New Yorkers could watch and hear the Duke of Iron, Lord Burgess, Johnny Barracuda, the Trinidad Steel Band, the Trinidancers, Massie Patterson, Lloyd Thomas and the Carib Dancers, and many others newly arrived from Trinidad's John John Hill.

From the other side of the world has come a lithe company of Asians. In 1934 Uday Shan-Kar showed America what native Hindu dancing was really all about, which was something of an embarrassment to Ruth St. Denis. In Shan-Kar's footsteps have come such Indian and Javanese dancers as Devi-Dja, Bhaskar, and Sasha.

Katherine Dunham and Pearl Primus have headlined a number of Negro and Afro-American programs since the late thirties, nor should we overlook Bill "Bojangles" Robinson,

194

a. Escudero

b. Bhaskar and Company

a. Calypso in Recital Hall

whose *A Tale of Old Africa* was a highlight of the spring of 1946. The National Negro Pageant Association annually brought to the Carnegie stage the best Negro dance talent in its company of actors, musicians, and dancers.

Great creative energy, expended in many different directions by many kinds of people, has characterized the dance story at Carnegie Hall. Occasionally there are pauses for contemplation and renewal. Virginia Lee of Ballet Arts reports, for example, that more students were signing up for classical training in the late fifties than for jazz or Hindu. The tempo of concert dance programs has slowed down. In 1961, aside from the small ANTA (American National Theatre & Academy) program in Recital Hall, the only dance event of any note was the Arthur Murray Dance Contest and Champions Exhibition—and even then. . . . In 1962, during the last season of the Philharmonic in Carnegie Hall, Andre Kostelanetz conducted the orchestra in an all-Tchaikovsky program featuring Patricia Wilde and Conrad Ludlow of the New York City Ballet in *Nutcracker* (the narrator: Ogden Nash).

"Not I, not I, but the wind that blows through me," wrote D. H. Lawrence on his function as a poet. This could well be the legend for a portrait of Carnegie Hall. The building—as a building—is an architectural curiosity. But the tempests of art, the winds of invention, the gusts and blasts of creative energy that have coursed through its halls, studios, and corridors have raised the Hall to heights of veneration. It is for Americans a substantial, tangible proof that ours is not just a nation—it is a civilization.

b. Calypso in Chapter Hall

196

(Opposite) Student rehearsing ballet annotated by Nimura in Ballet Arts Studio (61)

EPILOGUE

Epilogue

IF THERE WAS any doubt on July 1, 1960, when the Corporation took over Carnegie Hall, that the Hall could continue to be a major factor in the cultural life of both the city of New York and the country, that doubt has been permanently removed five years later. Figures alone do not reveal how needed the Hall is. New York must have Carnegie to maintain its standing as the musical capital of the world.

No one could have predicted it, but the applause that greeted the opening of Lincoln Center's Philharmonic Hall was partly drowned out in the uproar over its acoustics. This problem became one of Carnegie's unsought advantages. Though much has been done to alleviate acoustical difficulties at Philharmonic Hall, there is a deepening feeling of gratitude among both performers and audiences that Carnegie Hall still stands.

One of the first questions that the new management of the Hall had to face was how its income would be affected by the loss of the New York Philharmonic dates. As the main tenant of the Hall, the orchestra accounted for 120 dates each year.

The new group met this first grave problem with typical energy and forceful action. It resolved to change the Hall from a strictly rental operation. Today, Carnegie Hall not only rents its facilities; it also is an underwriter, promoter and presenter of its own events. Its aim is to present the very best artists in a variety of fields. During 1964 alone, Carnegie "produced" forty-five concerts in the Main Hall.

An outstanding example of this new policy is the Visiting Orchestra Series. It was developed by the tireless Executive Director Julius Bloom during the 1962–63 season, when three of the great orchestras of Europe, the Royal Philharmonic of London (Sir Malcolm Scott and Georges Pretre conducting), the Vienna Symphony (Wolfgang Sawallisch conducting) and the Philharmonia Hungarica (Mitiades Caradis conducting), all announced they would tour the United States that season. Bloom persuaded each of them to make a New York appearance at Carnegie Hall. He developed this as a subscription program and invited several American orchestras to come to New York to participate as well. The Visiting Orchestra Series is now a regular feature of each season.

Thus Carnegie Hall acts as impresario for, as well as providing a showcase for, the great orchestras of the world. They are brought to New York with the support of the J. M. Kaplan Fund, which helps to underwrite the trips, a cost which many of the groups could not bear themselves. This series gives Carnegie Hall a particularly attractive group of concerts, providing each season with that special excitement for which the Hall has long been famous.

One of the more recent developments at the Hall was originated by Chairman of the Board Frederick Richman to provide assistance for Carnegie's own production efforts. This is the Carnegie Hall Club. Its members are people who wish to help underwrite some of the programs undertaken by the Corporation, such as the student's reduced-rate ticket plan. This plan gives students the chance to buy top-priced seats for orchestral concerts through their schools at $2.50 each. The club helps make up the difference.

This sort of activity has given added impetus to the promotion of the concert-going habit with younger people. In the opinion of the Hall's directors it will help to foster a whole new generation of concert lovers, mature audiences who will recognize and appreciate the newer artists and help in launching promising careers. In perhaps no other area of its many endeavors has the Hall shown a greater concern over the development of young artists, as well as young ticket buyers, as with the Jeunesse Musicale.

This is a program begun in Belgium in 1943. It now has twenty-three member countries, the nucleus of a worldwide movement to make good music more readily available to young people by making artists, ensembles and speakers available to local chapters of member countries. The program also encourages gifted young artists through a system of awards and by means of regional, national and international exchange tours. In each member country the Jeunesse Musicale is a self-governing organization which adheres to certain fixed standards established by the International Federation, which charters local groups. The Ford Foundation has given a large grant to Carnegie Hall to help establish United States membership in Jeunesse Musicale on a nonprofit basis. Carnegie Hall will act as coordinator of activities and organizer of local chapters on four-year accredited college campuses and will represent the United States at international congresses. Exchange artists will make their debuts at Carnegie Hall and then tour the country, appearing at local chapters.

Carnegie's great reputation as a stage for the world has continued to make it a mecca for all sorts of performances. There has been greater flexibility in scheduling since the Philharmonic moved to its new quarters, and many managers have taken advantage of this to book their performers and events.

In 1962, the Columbia Broadcasting System made Carnegie Hall its sound stage for a television spectacular starring Julie Andrews and Carol Burnett. The Carnegie Hall setting lent a special glitter to that performance which helped make it a resounding hit. This was the first major use by television of the Hall, though there had been telethons based at Carnegie, as well as the famous Isaac Stern-Jack Benny show.

In the fall of 1962, the great German lieder singer Dietrich Fischer-Dieskau made his long-awaited debut in this country and received a tumultuous reception. In that year, the first for the Visiting Orchestra Series, Tony Bennett, Patachou, Charles Aznavour and the Limelighters also gave their all at Carnegie.

In 1963, Carnegie continued to increase its bookings and again displayed the amazing variety of events that has always been a characteristic. The American Jewish Congress held its Twentieth Anniversary of the Warsaw Ghetto meeting. Norman Mailer appeared and generated controversy. A young singer named Bob Dylan made his debut and immediately established himself as a major talent. The Moscow Chamber Orchestra appeared with Igor and David Oistrakh. And there were folk and jazz festivals in profusion.

Another interesting year was 1964. Two highlights were the Pablo Casals concert and the incredible first appearance in this country of four young Liverpudlians known as The Beatles. Their concert was a shattering experience for many New Yorkers. One result was a new policy: Carnegie Hall would no longer book rock-and-roll groups because of the apparent disregard of the audience for its own safety and well-being and the possibility of damage being done to the Hall itself.

All of this activity has destroyed public and private doubts about the future of Carnegie Hall. But, there was one event that eclipsed all others in its historic and musical importance in which the Hall played a major and vital role. And that was the return on May 9, 1965, of Vladimir Horowitz after a twelve-year absence from the concert stage.

It was known by a few people much before that date that Mr. Horowitz was contemplating giving a public performance. Julius Bloom, a trusted confidant of the pianist, arranged to have the Hall placed at Horowitz's disposal for rehearsal at any time. The main idea was to create as comfortable an atmosphere as possible so as to encourage the pianist as he sought to make the final decision about his return. A special Steinway was selected by Horowitz and brought to the Hall for the several rehearsals which took place. On each occasion there were twenty-five or thirty people, friends for the most part. And then one day the announcement was made that there would be a concert and that tickets would go on sale at the box office on Monday morning, April 26. The Sunday before was stormy, with strong winds and rain lashing the city through the night. As the storm raged, lines of music lovers began to form outside the Hall along 57th Street. By early morning the line stretched almost to Sixth Avenue, with more than 1500 eager ticket seekers watched by a special contingent of New York policemen brought to oversee the event.

The box office opened at ten o'clock, and in less than an hour all of the tickets put on sale had been purchased, leaving many people disappointed. Apparently a number of tickets had not been placed on sale but were held for notables and special friends of the pianist.

Even up to the very moment he was scheduled to come out on the stage there were some who expressed fears that Horowitz would not "go through with it." For the first time in Carnegie's eighty-four-year history not a single member of the audience was late. At three o'clock in the afternoon the houselights dimmed. There was not a sound. Then the great artist modestly walked to the center of the stage to be greeted by one of the most affectionate and prolonged bursts of applause ever heard in Carnegie. As he moved to the Steinway, the entire audience, as if rehearsed, became absolutely silent in unison and the concert began.

It was a great moment for Vladimir Horowitz, a great moment for Carnegie Hall and the people present and a great moment for the world. The pianist held everyone enthralled with his playing and created one of the most memorable events in the long history of the Hall. Fortunately, the concert was recorded, so many thousands will share this moment.

And so, Carnegie Hall has experienced a sort of renaissance. The uncertainty and anguish that enveloped it in 1960 has given way to a new joy and the hope of a future as bright as the past. For while the Hall echoes with the sounds of greatness, it also waits for future generations to come and pay homage, to laugh, to applaud, to argue, to be reverent, to come to the place where wonderful things will never stop happening.

A CARNEGIE
DISCOGRAPHY

A Carnegie Discography

Few public auditoriums are adequate for the recording of live performances that meet the standards of commercial sale. Carnegie Hall heads the list of those few. The leading recording companies rent both the main hall and Recital Hall for special recording sessions. (The Bunk Johnson revival actually began at such a recording session in Recital Hall in the early fifties.) They also record live performances in both hall, picking up the applause that follows. Carnegie is also one of the halls regularly wired by Voice of America for overseas broadcasts; hence, many countries abroad know of our cultural achievements principally through a Carnegie performance.

Recordings made by VOA are not available to the general public, but a generous library of commercial recordings is. It includes samples of the best of our classical and popular arts, with the applause of thousands of concertgoers. A few such long-playing records are listed below; those who have never visited Carnegie Hall can take their pleasure through "remote pickup" by playing one of these fine recordings.

Classical Music

Wilhelm Backhaus—Carnegie Hall Recital: 2-12"; London: LL-1108/9; a full evening of Beethoven, Brahms, Schubert, and Schumann are recorded in this handsome two-record set.

Jussi Bjoerling Sings at Carnegie Hall: 1-12"; RCA Victor: LM 2003; art songs and arias by one of the leading tenors of our day, recorded during a September, 1955, concert.

Vladimir Horowitz—*Pictures at an Exhibition:* 1-12"; RCA Victor: LM 2357; the excellent piano artist interprets the original Musorgski score during an April, 1951, concert.

David Oistrakh—Shostakovich Violin Concerto, Opus 99: 1-12"; Columbia: ML 5077; a distinguished performance by the great Russian violinist, with the New York Philharmonic under Dimitri Mitropoulos.

Van Cliburn—Rachmaninoff Concerto No. 3 in D Minor, Opus 30: 1-12"; RCA Victor: LM 2355 (also stereo); the historic homecoming concert, May 19, 1958, with Kiril Kondrashin conducting the Philharmonic.

Vladimir Horowitz—An Historic Return at Carnegie Hall: 2-12"; Columbia: M2L 328; a recording of the famous May 9, 1965, recital which brought the legendary virtuoso back from self-imposed seclusion into the limelight. The program includes works by Bach-Busoni, Scriabin and Chopin.

Verdi Requiem: 2-12"; RCA Victor: LM6018; Toscanini conducting the NBC Symphony with Herva Nelli, soprano, Fedora Barbieri, mezzo-soprano, Guiseppe de Stefano, tenor, Cesare Siepi, basso and the Robert Shaw Chorale conducted by Robert Shaw in a performance considered by many critics to be the greatest interpretation of this titanic work ever recorded.

Jazz Music

Diz 'n' Bird in Concert: 1-12"; Roost: 2234; this is a reissue of the September, 1947, concert that kicked off the era of big band bop.

Benny Goodman—Carnegie Hall Jazz Concert (complete): 2-12"; Columbia: OSL-160; from start to finish, the famous Goodman concert of 1938 that opened the hall to swing; also available in separate disks (CL-814, CL-815, and CL-816).

Woody Herman and the Herd at Carnegie Hall; 1-12"; Lion: L 70059; also a reissue of the original recording, made during Woody's great 1946 concert.

Mel Powell at Carnegie Hall: 1-12"; Columbia: CL-557; the sophisticated jazz pianist in a tasteful concert of new sounds.

Spring Street Stompers at Carnegie Hall: 1-12"; Jubilee: 1002; some two-beat doings for the benefit of a packed, enthusiastic audience.

Folk Music

Harry Belafonte at Carnegie Hall: 2-12"; RCA Victor: LOC 6006 (also stereo) ; the eminent singer at the height of his career in his first big Carnegie production, April, 1959.

Harry Belafonte Returns to Carnegie Hall: 2-12"; RCA Victor: LOC 6007 (also stereo) ; back for a second big event in 1960, this time assisted by the Belafonte Singers, Odetta, and Africa's star, Miriam Makeba.

Folk Song Festival at Carnegie Hall: 1-12"; United Artists: UAL 3050 (also stereo); the Alan Lomax extravaganza of 1959, featuring backwater blues and hoedowns by Muddy Waters, Jimmy Driftwood, Memphis Slim, and Stoney Mountain Boys.

Hootenannie at Carnegie Hall: 1-12"; Folkways: FW-FN 2512; Seeger, Hallie Wood, Tony Kraber, Reverend Gary Davis, and others singing out in a rousing hoot produced in September, 1959.

Odetta at Carnegie Hall: 1-12"; Vanguard: VRS 9076 (also stereo); a concert by the powerful voice of folk music's new generation, Odetta Felious.

Pete Seeger at Carnegie Hall with Sonny Terry: 1-12"; Folkways: FW-FA 2412; singer-banjoist-

guitarist Seeger holds forth in a December, 1957, concert, assisted by Sanford Sonny Terry, harmonicist nonpareil.

The Weavers at Carnegie Hall, Vol. 1: 1-12"; Vanguard: VRS 9010: for this concert the quartet consisted of Pete Seeger, Ronnie Gilbert, Lee Hays, and Fred Hellermann; recorded on Christmas Eve, 1955.

The Weavers at Carnegie Hall, Vol. 2: 1-12"; Vanguard: VRS 9075 (also stereo); Seeger is out and Erik Darling is in to share the four-part harmony, recorded April, 1960, in a supposed "farewell to Carnegie" concert.

Popular Music

Ted Heath at Carnegie: 1-12"; London: LL-1776; this is the big-band sound from England, in a program of well-scored standards.

Joni James at Carnegie Hall: 1-12"; M-G-M: E 3800 (also stereo); the personable pop singer, backed by a hundred strings, in a program of favorites recorded at her first Carnegie concert, May 2, 1959.

Glenn Miller Carnegie Hall Concert: 1-12"; RCA Victor: LPM 1506; the Miller band was in and out of Carnegie on many occasions; this record is an anthology of tunes recorded at the Hall at different times.

Miscellaneous

Paul Robeson at Carnegie Hall: 1-12"; Vanguard: VRS 9051 (also stereo); highlights from the newsmaking comeback concert of May, 1958; includes the *Othello* reading.

Two Cantors at Carnegie Hall: 1-12"; Tikva: T 52; comedian Eddie Cantor introduces Cantor Bela Herskovits in a concert of traditional Jewish music.

INDEX

Index

215

Photograph Credits

A Hall Is Built

P. 12 – a. BB b. CM; P. 13 – CM; P. 14 – a. The New York Historical Society; P. 15 – CM; P. 16 – BG; P. 17 – CM; P. 18 – BB; P. 19 – CM

Symphony Orchestras

P. 20 – a. Oratorio Society of New York; P. 20 (all) – BB; P. 23 – a. SS b. BB c. CR; P. 24 – a. SS b. CP c. BB d. RCA f. by Gray from Musical America; Pp. 25, 26-27 (all) – NBC Photos; P. 28 – a. SS b. RCA c., d., e. (last by Paul Schutzer) CR; P. 29 – BG; Pp. 30, 31 – CR; P. 32 – RCA; Pp. 33, 34 – CR; P. 35 – a. International News Photo b. CR; P. 36 – CR b. BG; P. 37 (all) – BB; Pp. 38, 39 (all) – RCA; P. 40 – CR; P. 41 – a. Conrad Eiger b., d. CR; P. 42 – a. CP b. AR; P. 43 – a. SS b. CR

The Lady of Fifty-Seventh Street

Burt Goldblatt

Prophets, Presidents & Protesters

P. 57 – b. BB; P. 58 (all) – O. Flaschner Music Company; P. 59 – a., b., d. BB e. BG; P. 60 – Theodore Roosevelt Association; P. 61 – Woodrow Wilson Foundation; P. 62 – b., c. BB; P. 63 (both) – BB; P. 64 – b. BB; P. 67 – a. BB b. International News Photo; P. 68 (both) – BB; P 69 – c. Jay Te Winburn; P. 70 – BB; P. 71 (both) – BG; P. 72 – Haven Studios courtesy of Felix G. Gerstman; P. 73 – Wide World

Solo Genius

P. 74 (all) – BG; P. 76 – CM; P. 77 – RCA; P. 78 – Felix G. Gerstman; P. 79 – a. BB
b. O. Flaschner Music Company; P. 80 – a. SS b. RCA, SS c. BB, SS; P. 81 – a. BB,
Columbia Artists Management, Inc. b. RCA c. SS; P. 83 – a. RCA b. Suzanne Szasz
courtesy of Esther Brown c. Lotte Meitner-Graf courtesy of Musical America
d. BB; P. 84 – RCA; P. 85 – SH; P. 86 (all) – BB; P. 87 – a. CM b., c. BB d. Renato
Toppo e. SH f. Bill Mark; P. 88 – SS; P. 90 – a. Whitestone Photo b. SS;
P. 91 – b. Adrian Siegel courtesy of SS; Pp. 92, 93 – CR; P. 94 – a. Black Star Photo
courtesy of RCA b. CR; P. 95 – a. Suzanne Szasz courtesy of Esther Brown b. AR;
P. 96 – Charles Rossi courtesy of SS; P. 97 – John G. Ross courtesy of RCA;
Pp. 98, 99 (both) – RCA; P. 100 – CR; P. 101 – a., c. SS b. CP; P. 104 – Adrian
Siegel courtesy of SS; P. 105 – a. Constantine Manos b. CR c. CP; P. 106 – a. CR;
P. 109 – b., c. CR; P. 110 – a., c. SS b. CM d. AR; P. 111 – a. CR b., f. AR c. BA
e. SS; P. 113 – SH

Intermission Stroll

Burt Goldblatt

Theater

P. 122 – BB; P. 125 (both) – BG; P. 126 – b. CM; P. 127 – a. AA b. Underwood and
Underwood c. CM; P. 128 (all) – AA; Pp. 129, 130 – BB; P. 131 – Theodore Karr
courtesy of Felix G. Gerstman; P. 133 – a. Amateur Comedy Club; P. 134
(both) – Amateur Comedy Club; P. 135 – BG; P. 136 – a. BG b. AA; P. 137 – BG;
P. 138 – a. BG; P. 139 – Felix G. Gerstman

Jazz

P. 140 – Henry Delorval Green; P. 143 – BG; P. 145 – b., c. MM; P. 146 – b. BG
c. Otto F. Hess courtesy of CR; P. 147 – a. M. Smith courtesy of MM b. MM;
P. 148 – a. MM b. Roger M. Stern courtesy of MM; P. 149 – a. Associated Booking
Corp. c. Libsohn-Ehrenberg courtesy of MM; P. 150 – CR; P. 151 – b. CR;
P. 152 – BG; P. 154 – b. BG; P. 155 (all) – BG; P. 156 – a. MM; P. 157 – Hauser
and Tischler; P. 159 – CP; P. 160 – Fred Plaut; P. 161 – BG

The Upper Floors

P. 162 – BB; P. 165 – BG; P. 166 – a. RCA b., c. BG; P. 167 – BG; P. 168 – a. Jas.
Abresch b. BG; P. 169 – a. Suzanne Szasz courtesy of Esther Brown b. BG

Ballads & Folk Songs

P. 170 – BG; P. 172 – Martin Harris; P. 174, 175 – RCA; P. 176 – a. BG c. Otto
F. Hess; Pp. 177, 178, 180 (both), 181, 182, 183 – BG

Dance

P. 184 – SH; P. 186 – BB; P. 187 – BA; P. 188 – a. BA b. BG; P. 189 – BA;
P. 190 – George Small courtesy of BA; P. 191 (both) – BA; Pp. 192, 193 – BG;
P. 195 – a. BG b. Art D'Lugoff Collection; P. 196 (both) – Art D'Lugoff Collection